Averting the SaaS Data Apocalypse

Averting the SaaS Data Apocalypse

The Role Data Protection Will Play in the Battle To Save Our Digital Future.

by **Simon Taylor**
Founder and CEO, HYCU

Averting the SaaS Data Apocalypse

To Vesa, who showed me the magic of making the impossible, possible; and to Enrique and Theresia, whose wisdom and heartfelt support helped transform vision into reality.

Table of Contents

Acknowledgements

This book and the journey we took to create the underlying vision it describes would not have been possible without the help of so many.

Thank you to Alexis Lope Bello, Jeff Williams, Stefan Cohen, Tim Daniels, BJ Jenkins, Andy Nallappan, Wendy Pfeiffer, Dheeraj Panday, Bob Almond, Andy Cohen, David Jones, Karim Nour, Julia Karol, Marija Zivanovic Smith, Jeff Carroll, Julie Rousseau-Shank, Mark Sutton, Laura Hilton, and all of the other members of my official and unofficial advisory boards over the years.

Thank you to Al Monserrat and Kevin Powers for empowering our team with guidance, outreach, advice, and training.

Thank you to the cadre of brilliant people and companies who have invested and supported HYCU including the teams at Bain Capital Ventures and Acrew Capital, Austin Arensberg from Okta Ventures, Sarah Hughes and Phil Braddock from Atlassian Ventures, and the teams at both Cisco Investments and Alpha Square Group, and everyone who took the time to meet with us, speak with us and get to know our story.

Thank you to our many partners and the people that saw something different in our approach and invested their personal time and effort to help us build something special: David Friend, Marty Falaro, Bill Andrews, Manvinder Singh, Tony Safoian, Emmanuel Benoit, thank you!

Thanks to Andrej Pavlovic, Peter Macquart, Taisto Bowers, Jeff Knutsen, Henry Helgeson, Chris Palmieri, Andrew Goldberg, Geoff Meyerson, Mike Fish, and Jason Aroesty.

Thank you to every HYCUer worldwide for your dedication, grit and belief in our ability to build a safer world. Endless thanks to Goran, Subbiah and Tanja for walking beside me on this journey from day one and to Schue and Coley for jumping aboard and embracing team purple. To Gary for throwing a HYCU license plate on his truck in the early days and Shreesha for his indomitable faith.

Thanks to our own Don Jennings and entrepreneurial wunderkind Matt Brown for working days and nights to edit, reduce and produce this book.

And finally, thank you to our readers, reviewers, and well-wishers: every critique, contribution, and clapping hand has shaped this tale.

With gratitude that overflows,
Simon

Foreword for "Averting the SaaS Data Apocalypse"

By Enrique Salem, Partner at Bain Capital

A New Age of Data Protection

In the swiftly changing realm of the digital era, businesses are navigating a world brimming with potential but also laden with intricate hurdles. This new environment, powered by technology, offers companies the promise of broader markets, more efficient operations, and innovative platforms to reach their clientele. The surge of the internet, mobile technology, and cloud computing has unlocked doors that were previously unimaginable. Enterprises can now engage with global audiences, employ remote teams, and leverage data-driven insights to make informed decisions.

However, with these opportunities come complexities that need deft maneuvering. One of the most urgent of these challenges lies in the domain of Software as a Service (SaaS). SaaS has transformed how businesses operate, offering cost-effective, scalable, and easily implementable solutions. From customer relationship management tools to enterprise resource planning systems, SaaS applications have embedded themselves deeply into the fabric of modern business operations.

Yet, the convenience of SaaS also brings with it concerns around data security. As companies entrust more of their critical data to third-party cloud applications, they grapple with ensuring that this data remains protected from breaches, loss, and unauthorized access. Beyond just the obvious security threats, there's the challenge of data sovereignty, compliance with an ever-evolving set of global data protection regulations, and the complexity of managing access across diverse user groups. The conundrum then is not just about leveraging the power of SaaS but doing so in a manner that prioritizes the sanctity and security of business-critical data.

From my early days in the startup realm to my time as the CEO of Symantec, I've been a first-hand witness to the explosive growth of data. This journey highlighted the crucial importance of data protection in contemporary times. Today, with an ever-increasing reliance on applications, businesses across scales use an array of tools and platforms for their day-to-day operations. This expansive utilization inevitably results in the creation of vast amounts of data, amplifying the need for meticulous and innovative data protection measures. As I've noted before, data volume continues to grow at an impressive rate, becoming a core concern for businesses globally.

Traditional backup mechanisms are often overwhelmed by the sheer volumes of daily data generation. This reality, combined with the vulnerabilities introduced by the rise of SaaS applications, accentuates the importance of a book like this.

HYCU, a Bain Capital Ventures Portfolio company, creates pioneering solutions, especially R-Cloud and data visualization tools like R-Graph. The company caters specifically to the unique challenges presented by SaaS data growth.

The intersection of artificial intelligence (AI) and our established data systems signifies one of the most promising, yet challenging terrains of the current technological epoch. AI, with its deep learning capabilities, predictive analytics, and automation, is reshaping industries, offering solutions that range from personalized user experiences to advanced data analytics and automation of repetitive tasks.

However, the promise of AI is not without its complexities. As more businesses venture into the AI arena, the magnitude of data being processed and generated is skyrocketing. Training AI models requires vast datasets to improve accuracy, and as these models learn and evolve, they produce even more data, further compounding the scale of information organizations manage.

This surge in data volume, in turn, accentuates the critical need for robust data protection strategies. In the age of breaches and cyber-attacks, the sheer volume of data generated by AI processes can present vulnerabilities. Moreover, when organizations incorporate their proprietary, often sensitive, data with widely available public AI models, they inadvertently create enticing opportunities for malicious actors. This juxtaposition of unique enterprise data with commonly accessible models can, if not adequately protected, provide potential entry points or become the 'Achilles heel' in an organization's data strategy.

Furthermore, as AI becomes increasingly integrated into business operations and decision-making processes, the reliability and integrity of the data feeding these systems become paramount. Any corruption or misinterpretation of this data can lead to flawed AI outputs, potentially causing significant operational or strategic errors.

While the fusion of AI with existing data infrastructures holds immense potential, it simultaneously demands a renewed emphasis on data protection and integrity. As we harness the power of AI, it's crucial to fortify our data protection mechanisms to safeguard the future of our digital ecosystems.

Simon Taylor, the forward-thinking CEO of HYCU, provides an in-depth exploration of this subject in "Averting the SaaS Data Apocalypse," presenting a thorough guide for readers. Simon's profound knowledge and perspectives, cultivated while leading an industry-shaping company, position this book as a must-read for anyone striving to understand the intricacies of contemporary data management.

"Averting the SaaS Data Apocalypse" is more than just a book; it is a beacon for businesses in these dynamic times. As we find ourselves at this pivotal juncture in the data revolution, comprehending, managing, and safeguarding our SaaS data becomes a paramount concern.

Simon Taylor's profound perspectives offer a blueprint for a more secure and streamlined digital age, ensuring the safeguarding of our digital tomorrow.

Enrique Salem.

Introduction: A Collision Course with Destiny

After the successful exit from my second company—a monitoring tools business sold to Citrix—I was ready for a break. I wanted to bask in the triumph, relish the satisfaction of a job well done. But destiny had other plans.

During a celebration with my partner, I bumped into Goran Garevski. He was immersed in something I considered dull and antiquated: data protection. How could something so humdrum be of any interest to a tech enthusiast like me?

But Goran challenged me. He saw something in data protection that I didn't—yet. Over dinner, he likened the state of data protection to taking a taxi when there was no Uber available. Data protection was a necessity, but where was the innovation? Where was the ease and accessibility? Where was the 'sexy' in this seemingly mundane field?

The Birth of an Idea: A Unified Platform for a Multi-Cloud World

Goran's words were intriguing. The night wore on, and the challenge of consumerizing data protection began

1

to take shape in our minds. SaaS, policy-driven, easy to use—these were the characteristics we envisioned. But it wasn't just about making data protection 'sexy.' We stumbled upon something greater—the equivalency problem.

We were living in a multi-cloud world with data silos scattered everywhere. Different companies offered protection for UNIX, Windows, VMware, but no single platform could cover it all. The nightmare of having hundreds of different backup products loomed large, and it was a terrible misuse of resources.

The solution? A unified platform to protect data across on-prem, public cloud, and SaaS environments with equivalent levels of support. This idea wasn't just a business opportunity; it was a call to arms in an age of digital sprawl.

The SaaS Revolution: Opportunities and Shadows

Our chance meeting in Las Vegas was the spark that ignited HYCU. Soon after, we were able to bring on Subbiah Sundaram to run our product team and together Goran, Subbiah and I dove furiously into building a new kind of data protection platform. But as we looked at the industry through this new, more modern lens we also gained a window into a broader world where SaaS was redefining everything. Businesses and individuals were falling in love with the convenience, flexibility, and power of SaaS applications.

Yet, behind the gleaming facade of this digital revolution, shadows were lurking. The same features that made SaaS enticing were also opening doors to cybersecurity risks and potential misuse. We quickly realized that the data protection platform of the future, the one we were endeavoring to build, would have to not only contend with, but revolutionize how people managed and protected SaaS data.

The SaaS Epoch: Embracing Innovation and Facing Hidden Challenges in the Digital Landscape

Over the past decade, technology has revolutionized our lives in ways we could have never imagined. The aftermath of the 2008 global economic crisis set the stage for massive investments in and the subsequent meteoric rise of Software-as-a-Service (SaaS) companies, transforming not only the way we live, work, and play but also the very essence of modern business operations. These ubiquitous SaaS companies, powered by brilliant software engineers scattered across the globe, now wield unparalleled influence, dictating everything from our fashion choices and favorite dining spots to our daily commute options to how we created visuals for business meetings and code for product development.

Embracing the seamlessness and convenience of SaaS, millions of individuals engage with business and consumer applications daily. We hop from ride-sharing apps to attend meetings at conferences to streaming services, relishing the user-friendly experience, and then seamlessly switch to our work tools, like Customer Relationship Management (CRM), Enterprise Resource Planning (ERP), and Business Intelligence (BI) solutions, among others. The allure of SaaS lies in its ability to simplify our lives and foster productivity, driving efficiency and innovation across industries.

Yet, as our team delved deeper into this burgeoning digital realm, we couldn't help but recognize the shadows lurking beneath its gleaming facade. Our obsession with understanding how SaaS impacted cyber security and data protection led us to the profound implications of entrusting our entire digital existence to faceless entities and relinquishing control of our data to locations beyond our reach.

In this book, we present the culmination of six years of research, unveiling the hidden risks concealed amidst the exponential growth of SaaS services. The very landscape that empowers businesses and consumers alike also presents formidable challenges that demand our attention. Our world has fallen in love with SaaS (and for good reason) embracing its transformative potential with open arms. However, it is equally crucial to grapple with the realities of security and privacy concerns that can put individuals and organizations at risk.

The World Needs and Loves SaaS: A Revolution of Accessibility and Innovation

The world's fervor for SaaS is driven by the unique advantages it brings to the table. SaaS has democratized access to advanced software and technology, tearing down barriers that once limited businesses and individuals. With the rise of SaaS, even startups and small businesses can leverage sophisticated tools without a massive upfront investment. This democratization has fueled entrepreneurship and innovation, allowing nimble companies to compete on a global scale.

Moreover, the cloud-based nature of SaaS enables unprecedented scalability and flexibility. Organizations can swiftly adapt to evolving market demands, easily scaling their operations up or down as needed. The collaborative nature of SaaS applications also fosters seamless teamwork, regardless of geographical barriers, empowering global workforces to collaborate and create.

SaaS has undoubtedly become an indispensable component of modern-day business operations, fueling productivity, accelerating digital transformation, and driving economic growth.

The Shadow Side: Cybersecurity Risks in the SaaS Era

As the saying goes, with great power comes great responsibility, and the SaaS revolution is no exception. The very characteristics that make SaaS enticing also expose organizations to cybersecurity risks. Entrusting sensitive data to external vendors introduces a degree of uncertainty, as organizations must rely on the security practices of these third-party providers.

One pressing concern is the potential for data breaches and unauthorized access to sensitive information. While reputable SaaS providers invest heavily in security measures, no system is impervious to determined cybercriminals. An incident involving a widely used SaaS application could have far-reaching consequences, impacting multiple organizations and users simultaneously.

Furthermore, the decentralized nature of SaaS brings forth a potential attack surface that is hard to monitor and control. Cyber attackers are increasingly capitalizing on SaaS applications as a vector to infiltrate organizations. They leverage legitimate tools to carry out phishing attacks, deploy malware, or execute ransomware campaigns, amplifying the risks that businesses face.

Two Ransomware Attacks Executed through SaaS

1. Cloud Hopper (PwC, 2017): A notorious cyber espionage campaign executed through SaaS applications was discovered in 2016. The Cloud Hopper attack targeted managed service providers (MSPs) to gain unauthorized access to their clients' networks. By infiltrating MSPs, the attackers could breach multiple organizations through a single entry point. The campaign affected numerous high-profile companies, illustrating the potential cascading effect of a SaaS-related attack.

2. WastedLocker (Malware Bytes, 2020): In 2020, the WastedLocker ransomware wreaked havoc on organizations worldwide. This attack exploited vulnerabilities in a SaaS cloud infrastructure to infiltrate targeted networks, encrypting critical data and demanding ransom payments. The incident highlighted the risks associated with interconnected cloud ecosystems, where an attack on one organization can have a ripple effect on others.

Navigating the Future: Balancing SaaS Benefits and Cybersecurity Vigilance

As the SaaS revolution continues to reshape our digital landscape, it is imperative for businesses to strike a delicate balance between embracing the transformative power of SaaS and safeguarding their digital fortresses. Vigilance and proactivity are key in fortifying data protection measures, working in tandem with SaaS providers to bolster security protocols.

In the following chapters, we embark on a compelling journey that sheds light on the dance between SaaS, cybersecurity and data protection. By understanding the unseen threats that underpin our daily interactions with technology, we can fortify our data's sanctity and seize the boundless opportunities that SaaS offers.

Averting the SaaS Data Apocalypse

This book isn't just a chronicle of HYCU's journey or a simple business story. It's a complex tapestry that weaves the promise, potential, and perils of the SaaS era. From the inception of an idea over a steak dinner to the realization of a platform serving thousands of customers across 78 countries, it's a narrative filled with insights, lessons, and warnings.

We'll explore the unique challenges of data protection, the nuances of cybersecurity in the SaaS era, and the urgent need for a new approach that balances innovation with responsibility.

Join me, Simon Taylor, as we venture into this uncharted territory, armed with the conviction and curiosity that led me from that celebratory toast in Las Vegas to the front lines of averting a potential SaaS data apocalypse.

Your guide on this journey,
Simon Taylor
Founder & CEO, HYCU

*The future is here, but are we ready?
Let's find out together.

**Scan this QR Code to find out what SaaS data
you may have unprotected with R-Graph.**

CHAPTER 1

The Dawn of the SaaS Data Apocalypse

The Golden Era of CIOs

In the dawn of the 21st century, the role of Chief Information Officer (CIO) was distinctively different than it is today. The primary focus was on managing the technology and systems within the business while facilitating a smoother digital transition. My father, as the CIO of a leading financial services company, was among the pioneers who charted the course of this change. Armed with a billion-dollar operating budget, he efficiently managed the company's vast technology infrastructure, making strategic IT investments and decisions, and set the foundation for the digitization of operations.

As a recognized leader in his field, my father's exceptional management skills led to him being recognized as one of the Wall Street Journal's top 20 CIOs of his generation. At that time, the data environment was less convoluted, with information contained in five or six silos.

The siloed nature of data meant there were limited integration concerns, and data management was primarily about storage and retrieval. Data security issues were crucial even then, but the threats were not as widespread or as sophisticated as they are today. Today there is a ransomware attack every 11 seconds with statistics showing that by 2031 attacks will occur every 2 seconds. (11 Seconds, 2021)

However, the seemingly well-structured data world was not without its challenges. Although data silos ensured a degree of security and simplicity, they often resulted in redundant data storage and a lack of holistic view across different business operations. The cost of maintaining physical data servers was also a significant concern, and server failures could lead to catastrophic data losses. Despite these challenges, CIOs, including my father, managed to effectively steer their companies through these challenges, laying the groundwork for the data-driven enterprises we see today.

Yet, as is the nature of technology, change was on the horizon. The next fifteen years saw a significant shift in the way businesses managed and utilized data. The age of multi-siloed data was slowly giving way to a new era that would drastically alter the role of the CIO, the structure of data management, and the overall business landscape.

The Tectonic Shift: Data Dispersal and the Rise of SaaS

Just a few years down the line from the era of my father, the universe of data took a dramatic turn. The last ten years has brought forth a seismic shift in the data landscape. The rise of SaaS was at the heart of this change. The consolidation of data within five or six silos became a thing of the past. The introduction of SaaS led to an explosion of data silos, with the average company's data now scattered across as many as 217 different silos.

The emergence of SaaS solutions came as a part of the broader digital transformation trends. As cloud technology matured, it brought forth a more convenient, efficient, and cost-effective way of managing data and running applications. A decade earlier, the rise of public cloud platforms like AWS, Google Cloud, and Azure marked the beginning of this shift. They opened up the possibilities of scaling up or down the IT resources as per the business needs without worrying about the infrastructure management.

The same set of challenges that Virtualization had thrust upon us were now intensified and amplified with the advent of SaaS. It was as if IT administrators were playing a high-speed game of digital whack-a-mole, spinning up Virtual Machines (VMs) in a dizzying array of directions. This frantic digital ballet led to an unpredictable, wild sprawl of VMs, akin to urban expansion, with more data than we had ever seen before left in the cold, unprotected, or worse, lost in the ether, forever unretrievable. So, it wasn't merely a case of data dispersal scattershot across the digital universe, but also a symptom of the relentless, ever-evolving emergence of grand technological shifts that are redefining our world.

Simultaneously, the introduction of SaaS solutions like Salesforce and G-Suite (now Google Workspace) further drove this transformation. SaaS offered businesses the convenience of using software over the internet on a subscription basis. It eliminated the need for companies to install and run applications on their own computers or in their data centers.

However, this boon came with its set of challenges. One of the most significant was data dispersal. As businesses adopted multiple SaaS applications, their data began spreading across different places. This scattering of data was not just within their own controlled environments but also extended to third-party platforms managed by SaaS providers. In an attempt to simplify processes and reduce costs, companies inadvertently relinquished control over their data.

This emergence and proliferation towards SaaS applications and platforms, along with the associated data dispersal, had profound implications. It fundamentally changed how businesses operate, how they manage their data, and, most importantly, how they protect their data. Little did we know, this transition was creating a setup ripe for chaos. The stage was set for what I've come to call the SaaS Data Apocalypse.

The Deceptive Allure of SaaS: Convenience vs Control

The rise of SaaS was driven by a promise of simplicity. Organizations relished the thought of merely turning on a service rather than having to download, install, and maintain an entire software product. The thought of having sophisticated, high-powered software platforms managed entirely by a third-party vendor was too appealing to ignore. These products were aesthetically pleasing, functionally superior, and promised an era of smooth, hassle-free software usage. Companies were drawn to the allure of SaaS. The assumption was that everything, from infrastructure to data management and even data security, would be taken care of by the SaaS providers. This idea was called the shared responsibility model for data protection.

In a bid to simplify operations, businesses worldwide enthusiastically adopted numerous SaaS applications. From sales to customer relationship management, from human resources to project management, there was a SaaS solution for everything. And these solutions weren't just being adopted; they were being used extensively, housing mission-critical data, and powering essential business processes.

However, as with any major technological transition, the shift towards SaaS came with its set of unforeseen challenges. One of the biggest and least anticipated issues was the perceived immunity from data threats. As the number of SaaS vendors grew, so did the belief that all data, once handed over to these vendors, would be safeguarded magically.

In reality, the shift to SaaS was luring businesses into a false sense of security. Businesses started to believe that their data was secure in the hands of their SaaS vendors. This fallacy was the beginning of an IT catastrophe waiting to happen. It was a baited trap for organizations, making them believe that their data was being taken care of by someone else when, in fact, it wasn't.

Thus, while SaaS providers continued to reel in businesses with promises of simplicity and ease of use, the stark reality was quite different. The trade-off between convenience and control was far from clear, and the shift toward SaaS was placing organizations in a precarious position. It was leading us closer to the precipice of a data disaster.

The Harsh Reality: Unprotected Data and Vulnerability

As businesses danced to the siren song of SaaS, a chilling reality was overlooked - the illusion of data protection. The common belief was that the data stored in the public cloud, or a SaaS application was inherently protected and recoverable. The reality, however, was entirely different.

Under the shared responsibility model adopted by most SaaS services and cloud platforms, the vendors are responsible for the security of their infrastructure. In contrast, the responsibility of securing the data itself lies with the customers. This often-misunderstood delineation of responsibilities has resulted in an alarming 77% of the world's data being left vulnerable (Key Findings SaaS Management, 2022). This vulnerability extends to threats from ransomware attacks, accidental data loss, and other cybersecurity threats.

The magnitude of this issue can be understood in the light of two significant trends. On one hand, offensive cyber capabilities such as ransomware and cyber terrorism have become more accessible, cheaper, and simpler. On the other hand, the complexity of IT environments and their corresponding defensive capabilities have significantly increased.

This creates a "perfect storm" for a cyber disaster. Today, more than half of all companies have experienced a ransomware attack via SaaS (Odaseva, 2022), and a majority of these attacks have been successful. This isn't because people have become less intelligent or cautious. Instead, it is because data is now scattered across more places than ever before, making it increasingly difficult to secure.

Furthermore, there's a pervasive myth that the data protection responsibility lies with the SaaS providers, causing companies to ignore the problem. However, the reality is that the responsibility of securing data lies with the companies themselves. This collective denial and ignorance of data responsibility is one of the fundamental problems of our digital age.

The Dire Consequences: A Call to Action

The dire consequences of leaving data unprotected in the new age of SaaS are hard to ignore. Every successful ransomware attack brings to light the high stakes we're dealing with. The situation is made graver because we are not dealing with just corporate losses or financial impacts.

The fallout of our lax approach to data security has seeped into mission-critical infrastructure, impacting essential services and endangering lives. One recent example that stands out is the ransomware attack on August 3rd, 2023, on the Eastern Connecticut Health Network (ECHN) and Waterbury HEALTH, part of Prospect Medical Holdings, which caused significant disruption to healthcare delivery within 19 towns served by healthcare entities. (FBI investigating ransomware attack affecting Eastern Connecticut Health Network, Waterbury HEALTH, 2023)

Numerous services, including elective surgeries and outpatient laboratories, were forced to shut down. Waterbury HEALTH's computer systems were shut down, affecting all inpatient and outpatient operations, leading to rescheduling of appointments and a shift to paper records. This attack, showcases the horrifying potential of what a cyber-attack on a critical institution looks like, taking the threat of cyber warfare from the realm of the abstract to a devastating reality.

The landscape of modern warfare is changing, and we are witnessing a shift towards cyber warfare. Whether it's a pregnant woman trapped on a bridge due to traffic lights shut down by a cyber-attack or gas stations unable to supply fuel, the implications are widespread and terrifying. Data vulnerability has the potential to disrupt societies, economies, and our everyday lives.

It is clear that we are entering a new era, an era where data security and data protection are the front lines of our defense. As a society, we need to acknowledge the importance of this issue and take collective action to address it. The first step in doing so is dispelling the myth that data in the cloud or with a SaaS provider is inherently safe.

The harsh reality is that companies must take responsibility for protecting their data. The misconception that SaaS providers are taking care of their data security needs to be debunked. We need to spread the message that SaaS providers are in the business of providing a service, not protecting individual companies' data.

If we continue to ignore this issue, we run the risk of exposing ourselves to increasingly frequent and severe attacks. We have a collective responsibility to protect our data, our institutions, and, ultimately, our society.

Looking Ahead: The Key Role of HYCU and CIOs in Safeguarding Data

As we navigate through the complex landscape of SaaS and data dispersal, it becomes increasingly clear that a proactive and informed approach is necessary. This is where HYCU and the strategic role of Chief Information Officers (CIOs) come into play.

HYCU is an industry-leading and visionary SaaS data backup and recovery solutions provider. The company is ideally positioned to offer practical solutions to these data-related challenges. Leveraging the best-in-class technology and deep understanding of modern IT environments, HYCU empowers businesses to protect their data effectively.

But HYCU can't do it alone. The CIOs, who are responsible for an organization's IT strategy, play a pivotal role in overcoming these challenges. The growing complexity and diversity of IT environments demand that CIOs evolve their roles from being mere technology managers to becoming business strategists and educators. This transformation is vital in navigating the SaaS landscape effectively and securely.

In this book, we will delve deeper into actionable strategies and steps that CIOs can take to safeguard their data. We will debunk myths, equip you with the knowledge to ask the right questions, and help you understand the shared responsibility model. We will guide you through understanding the potential pitfalls of SaaS adoption without a robust data protection strategy, and how to avoid them.

The future chapters of this book will introduce CIOs to the essential tools and strategies needed to safeguard their organizations' data and become part of the solution, not the problem. It will help CIOs master the modern data landscape, with an emphasis on data protection in the SaaS era. Practical case studies, best practices, and actionable tips will empower CIOs to become the frontline warriors in the fight against data vulnerability.

As we move forward in the SaaS data apocalypse, remember, protecting data is not just about securing bits and bytes. It's about safeguarding the lifelines of our modern societies, our businesses, and our lives. It's time for us to join forces in understanding, taking action, and transforming this challenge into an opportunity for a safer and more secure digital future. It's time to for us to avert the SaaS Data Apocalypse.

Are you prepared to recover from a ransomware attack?

Scan this QR code to find out what your R-Score is today!

CHAPTER 2

The Problem of Our Time

In the past decade, the SaaS industry has seen explosive growth. Currently, there are an estimated 23,000 SaaS vendors worldwide (Number SaaS Companies Statatistics, 2023), a number that keeps ticking upwards with each passing day. This sheer volume represents the transformation of the digital business landscape, driven by a shift to cloud-based applications and services.

As a CEO in the data protection industry, I've had the unique opportunity to observe this dynamic shift unfold in real-time. However, with this unprecedented growth in SaaS services, one must question the potential risks associated. With my team at HYCU, we sought to uncover the magnitude of this issue by leveraging well-respected industry resources such as Gartner.

For those who may be unaware, Gartner is a globally recognized research and advisory firm that businesses across the world rely on to make informed decisions. One of their widely used tools is the Gartner Magic Quadrant. This annual research report provides a graphical competitive positioning of four types of technology providers, in markets where growth is high, and provider differentiation is distinct.

These Magic Quadrants are often seen as the de facto yardstick in the industry, offering a deep dive into who's who and their standing in terms of market impact. For us, it was an essential starting point to gauge the state of data protection amongst SaaS vendors. We went through the 2022 Magic Quadrant for Enterprise Backup and Recovery Software Solutions, a category that we ourselves are proud to be a part of.

Our research led us to a shocking discovery. Among the 23,000 SaaS vendors globally, only five of them were backed up and recoverable via the world's leading data protection vendors. Not five percent, but five. Just five vendors. (Gartner Magic Quadrant for Enterprise Backup and Recovery Software Solutions , 2023).

This fact, in and of itself, was astounding. It was a stark reminder that while the SaaS industry is booming, a significant majority of these vendors were not adequately protected against data loss. They weren't prepared for a recovery scenario, rendering them and their users vulnerable to data breaches and losses.

Our discovery raised some significant questions. With 23,000 SaaS vendors and counting, why were only five protected by the leading data protection providers? What risks did this massive gap pose to organizations relying on these SaaS vendors? As we delved deeper into these issues, we began to realize the magnitude of what we were up against – a potential SaaS data apocalypse. And we knew it was imperative to shed light on this impending issue, lest we find ourselves unprepared for a disaster of an unprecedented scale.

Understanding the Gap

One might wonder, why such a significant gap in data protection among SaaS vendors? There must be reasons, after all, they can't all be careless or unaware, right? As a CEO in this sector, I can assure you that it's not for a lack of trying or knowledge. Rather, it's the approach that most backup vendors have traditionally taken, one silo at a time.

Consider the history of data protection. Each major player in the backup vendor market was born out of a specific need. Veritas came into existence because there was a need to back up UNIX. Commvault was established when Windows needed to be backed up. And then there was Veeam, a response to the need to backup VMware.

The issue with this approach is its inherent limitation - each platform built a solution for a particular need, a specific silo. What happened when these platforms attempted to venture outside their initial silos? Unfortunately, their attempts to diversify often fell short. They weren't able to replicate their success across other platforms or silos effectively or without introducing complexity.

At HYCU, we recognized this issue and sought to take a different route. Our goal was to build something more comprehensive, a solution that would be effective across all these diverse platforms and silos. We saw the need for a heterogeneous solution, one that could serve the backup and recovery needs of the 23,000 SaaS vendors and more.

To validate this new approach and understand its potential impact, we turned to industry leaders and decision-makers. One such individual was Mark Sutton, the Chief Information Security Officer for Bain Capital. He saw our solution and instantly recognized its potential. He called it the "problem of our time."

Bain Capital, managing billions of dollars in funds, understands the stakes involved with data protection. Mark Sutton saw that our solution wasn't just an improvement, it was a necessity. It filled a gap that didn't have an existing solution, providing a way to see and protect all data, irrespective of where it was located.

This validation from a leader at Bain Capital underscored the urgency and importance of the issue. But it wasn't just the financial sector that realized this; the need for comprehensive data protection was being recognized across industries and institutions.

Take, for instance, the Boston College Cybersecurity Conference, where I had the privilege to speak as a keynote speaker alongside Federal, law enforcement, academic and industry leaders including FBI Director Christopher Wray. Director Wray, in particular, emphasized the need for reliable data backup and recovery systems. The FBI, the White House, and even the legislation was all echoing the same sentiment – the need for thorough data protection was more crucial than ever before (Data Privacy White House Government, 2022).

However, the key point that many seemed to miss was the definition of data itself. Data isn't limited to what's stored in your local servers or even in your cloud storage. Data includes everything you use to run your organization, wherever it may be. It's all-encompassing, and its protection should be too.

In essence, we need to tackle the shared responsibility model, where SaaS vendors provide the service but relinquish responsibility for data protection and recovery. Recognizing this, and acting upon it, is crucial for averting a potential SaaS data apocalypse.

The Threats Are Real

The looming threats to SaaS data are not theoretical. They are real, palpable, and have the potential to inflict catastrophic damage. Every day, businesses across the globe face numerous cyber threats. As I already mentioned, according to the World Economic Forum (Global Cyber Outlook, 2023), the probability of a major enterprise data breach is now over 29%, and it's predicted to keep rising. But where are these threats coming from?

We have always considered external threats like hackers and cybercriminals as the primary source of data breaches. However, recent findings by Netwrix (Hybrid Security Trends, 2023), a cybersecurity company, show that almost half of all data breaches were caused by internal factors. Surprising, right?

These internal breaches are typically attributed to negligent or malicious employees. But that's not the whole story. The internal threat landscape is far more complex and includes not just negligent or disgruntled employees, but also issues stemming from employee churn, departures, and simple, human error.

Take an example of employee churn. In many SaaS applications, when an employee leaves an organization, their account often remains active. This leaves a gateway open for potential breaches, which can lead to data loss or compromise. This is a real and significant threat, which, unfortunately, most companies fail to address.

Another frequent cause of data loss is plain human error. Misconfiguration of cloud services is a prevalent issue that leads to data breaches. Gartner estimates that through 2025, a staggering 99% of cloud security failures will be the customer's fault (Is the Cloud secure?, 2019).

Imagine for a moment, an engineer who is new to a project and is working late. They accidentally delete a dataset, and with that single mistake, years of valuable data could be gone. A moment of oversight or confusion can lead to catastrophic data loss (Hybrid Security Trends, 2023).

Then there are third-party apps. In today's interconnected world, third-party apps have become ubiquitous. Yet, they present another significant threat. If you think about the modern digital ecosystem, it's rife with third-party apps that integrate with SaaS platforms. Each app presents a new potential entry point for a data breach.

Now, let's talk about SaaS providers. Their main focus is to ensure uptime, availability, and continuity of service. Their focus and resources are spent improving their own service and not on data protection. And why is that? Because their DevOps teams are continuing to look to add new features and functions on the services they provide. Their focus is less on the data management or data protection. That is the customer's responsibility. This creates a situation where the onus of data protection falls on the customer, not the provider. A shift in this mindset is crucial.

Even traditional security measures like firewalls and intrusion detection systems (IDS) can't guarantee complete data protection or even recovery in the SaaS environment. They are unable to address internal threats and are often blind to the more subtle and insidious forms of breaches that are increasingly becoming the norm.

It's imperative to understand and acknowledge that the threats are real. They come from a multitude of sources and are constantly evolving. To combat them, we need to evolve our defenses as well, taking a holistic approach to data protection.

The Solutions Are Not Adequate

For far too long, we've trusted in traditional solutions to protect our data, believing that it's enough to keep the threats at bay. Sadly, this belief couldn't be farther from the truth. We need to come to terms with the reality that the solutions we've relied upon are no longer adequate.

Think about backup and recovery solutions, one of the most trusted lines of defense against data loss. In the past, regular backups have saved many businesses from potential ruin. However, in the rapidly evolving SaaS environment, traditional backup solutions and methods are becoming less effective.

Why is that? Well, first and foremost, the scale of data has significantly increased. Backing up terabytes or even petabytes of data daily or weekly is time consuming and costly. It's not just about the sheer volume of data, though; the complexity is an equally challenging aspect. The data in the modern SaaS environment is intricately linked and constantly changing. A single backup can't keep up with these rapid changes and may fail to fully capture the complex web of interlinked data.

On top of that, traditional backup solutions typically involve a long and often complex recovery process. In an era where businesses need to be agile and responsive, lengthy recovery times can cause significant disruption and financial losses. What's more, traditional backup systems don't offer the granular recovery options required in the SaaS environment. Often, it's not the entire dataset that's lost or corrupted but specific files or folders. Being forced to recover the entire dataset just to retrieve a single file is inefficient and frustrating.

And let's not forget about the insider threats that I mentioned earlier. Traditional backup solutions were designed to protect against external threats, not internal ones. They are unable to address the complex threat landscape where negligent or disgruntled employees, employee churn, misconfigurations, and third-party apps can lead to data breaches.

What about disaster recovery plans? Yes, they are essential, and they can help recover data in case of catastrophic incidents. But they are not foolproof. For one, disaster recovery plans are usually focused on recovering from major incidents like natural disasters or cyberattacks, not the small-scale incidents that are more common in the SaaS environment. Also, they don't offer real-time data protection, leaving a significant gap that could lead to data loss.

Lastly, there's a common misconception that SaaS providers are responsible for data protection. As I pointed out earlier, this is not true. In today's IT environments, the responsibility of data protection falls on the customer, not the provider. Many businesses hope that their SaaS providers will protect their data, leaving them vulnerable to data loss. As we all know, hope has never been an effective strategy for anything, especially data protection.

So, what's the solution then? How can businesses protect their data in this complex and evolving landscape? It's clear that a new approach is needed, one that goes beyond traditional solutions and addresses the unique challenges posed by the SaaS environment. We need solutions that offer real-time protection, granular recovery options, protection against internal threats, and most importantly, easy, quick and effective recovery. Only then can businesses confidently navigate the SaaS environment without fear of data loss.

The Urgent Need for a SaaS Data Defense

In the face of this looming SaaS data apocalypse, the need for robust, holistic, and proactive data protection strategies cannot be overemphasized. Enterprises and organizations need to move beyond the prevailing shared responsibility model and take full ownership of their data security across all silos. This shift requires an overarching strategy that spans all data sources and considers every SaaS service as a potential entry point for ransomware attacks.

This level of protection is currently missing in a vast majority of businesses. The astonishing figures mentioned earlier – more than 23,000 SaaS services globally, yet only five adequately protected – underscores the scope of the challenge we face. It's a gaping hole in our defenses, making our data and operations highly vulnerable.

It's time for businesses to shatter the myth that SaaS data is inherently safe. Many SaaS vendors explicitly state they are not responsible for data protection or recovery. However, a common misconception persists that SaaS data is immune to loss or theft. This complacency is dangerous. Businesses must acknowledge that the data they use to operate their organizations, wherever it may be, is their responsibility.

Add the rapid advancements in AI to the equation, and the urgency for robust data protection becomes even more critical. AI, particularly generative AI, is poised to make the execution of ransomware attacks significantly easier and cheaper, leading to an increase in the frequency and scale of these threats. The challenge for enterprises is twofold: dealing with the explosion of data silos and the diminishing costs of offensive cyber capabilities.

The problems highlighted in this book are indeed the "problems of our time." They represent a significant existential threat to businesses globally, impacting not just individual organizations, but economies and societies at large. As I have pointed out, the task now is to equip businesses with the tools, knowledge, and mindset necessary to prevent the SaaS data apocalypse.

In the end, the value of data is incalculable. It's the lifeblood of modern businesses, governments, and institutions. Protecting it should be one of our highest priorities. The SaaS data apocalypse is not an inevitability. It's a potential future that we can, and should, strive to prevent. By understanding the scope of the challenge, acknowledging our shared responsibility, and taking decisive steps to protect our data, we can navigate towards a safer, more secure digital future.

Scan this QR Code to find out what SaaS data you may have unprotected with R-Graph.

CHAPTER 3

The SaaS Data Nightmare

In today's fast-paced business environment, SaaS applications have undeniably reshaped how companies function. The digital revolution, spearheaded by this class of software, has simplified operational complexities, ensuring that businesses, whether startups or multinational conglomerates, can pivot and adapt with agility to ever-changing market dynamics. A firm in San Francisco, for example, can effortlessly collaborate with its team in Singapore or London, thanks to the cloud infrastructure that SaaS platforms offer. Meetings, data analytics, and even intricate project management tasks have been translated into seamless digital experiences.

Their versatility and efficiency, however, come at a price. As with any major shift, the ripple effects have both positive and negative consequences. While the positives are numerous and apparent, from cost savings to increased flexibility, the negative repercussions are subtle and, often, only become discernible with time. SaaS has allowed for a democratization of software access, enabling even non-technical departments to integrate tools that serve their needs without waiting for lengthy procurement or installation processes.

With rapid adoption across various departments, there emerges an unforeseen dilemma. Data - that invaluable resource businesses have come to rely upon in the information age - is no longer housed within the physical confines of an organization's IT infrastructure. Instead, it finds itself dispersed, strewn across a multitude of platforms, from CRM tools to marketing automation software and collaborative workspaces. Each department, in its bid for efficiency, may integrate tools of its choice, leading to a scenario where critical company data is spread thin across the digital universe.

The very essence of our modern society is built on data. It's the bedrock upon which our digital civilization has been constructed. From how we communicate and work to how we live and learn - everything is intertwined with data. Software as a Service (SaaS), a term now ubiquitous in our business lexicon, is at the heart of this digital evolution.

Yet, as much as SaaS has been a boon to efficiency and growth, it also introduces a new set of risks that are alarmingly significant. We're standing at the precipice of what I refer to as the SaaS data apocalypse. It's not a doomsday prophecy or an exaggerated nightmare. It's not an abstract idea confined to the theoretical musings of a dystopian novel. Rather, it's a real and present danger, a current event unfolding right before our eyes. The world we live in is at risk.

The SaaS data apocalypse is happening, here and now. It's the shadow cast by the brilliant light of technology, a specter looming ever larger with each passing day. And the ramifications of this scenario are unimaginable, both for businesses that form the economic backbone of our society and the society at large.

As I sit here writing this chapter, I do so with a sense of urgency and an obligation to shine a light on this pressing issue. It's a problem that's insidious in its complexity and global in its reach. And much like the climate crisis or a pandemic, it's a threat that doesn't discriminate between sectors, industries, or nations.

In our highly digital world, data is more than a commodity. It's an indispensable resource, a lifeblood that sustains our societies, economies, and, in many ways, our very way of life. And like any other valuable resource, it attracts attention, often the wrong kind. SaaS platforms, repositories of vast amounts of valuable data, have inevitably become targets for malicious actors.

It's not hard to understand why. The convenience, scalability, and efficiency offered by SaaS are also its greatest vulnerabilities. The sheer scale of data handled by these services and the widespread reliance on them have painted a bulls-eye on their backs. It's not a question of "if" but "when" a serious breach will occur, with potentially catastrophic consequences.

Think about it - from small businesses managing their accounting to multinational corporations handling terabytes of sensitive customer data, SaaS has become an integral part of our business operations. Government agencies, healthcare systems, educational institutions - the list goes on. All are increasingly reliant on SaaS, which means the ripple effects of a SaaS data apocalypse will be felt far and wide.

As we advance further into the age of digitalization, the potential fallout from such a catastrophe only grows larger. It's a ticking time bomb, and the clock is rapidly winding down. We cannot afford to ignore this issue, nor can we afford to be complacent. The time to act is now.

I often reflect on the weight of this realization and the responsibility it brings. As the CEO of HYCU, a company deeply involved in data protection, I'm privy to the darker underbelly of our digital world. I've seen firsthand how the promise of technology can be subverted, turning a tool for progress into a weapon of disruption. It's a sobering reality, but it's one we must face head-on.

The Worst-Case Scenario: The Vulnerable at Risk

In the context of the SaaS data apocalypse, we must brace ourselves to envision the unthinkable. To fully grasp the gravity of this issue, let's cast our eyes toward the darkest corners of the possible. And make no mistake, these aren't distant, implausible scenarios, but a real and probable future if our approach to data security remains complacent.

Imagine a world, much like our own, where data breaches extend beyond the business realm, piercing through the very fabric of our daily lives, to impact those most defenseless - our children, our elderly, our sick, our needy. Consider the vulnerability of those for whom a SaaS data breach would carry life-altering consequences.

Consider an average day at a school, a hospital, a community center. Our children, our future, are using SaaS applications for their learning, their play, their growth. Suddenly, a data breach brings everything to a halt. A child's sensitive personal information, once secured, now lies exposed. Teachers, unable to access their lesson plans, struggle to maintain a semblance of normalcy amidst the ensuing chaos. It's an unsettling picture. But it gets worse.

Now, picture a child going into surgery. The doctors, nurses, and anesthesiologists depend on a SaaS system to retrieve critical medical records, to manage operating schedules, to control life-sustaining equipment. Suddenly, the system fails. There's no warning, no time to prepare. The hospital is thrown into chaos, and the child, the innocent bystander in this catastrophe, bears the brunt of it. A heart-wrenching scenario, isn't it? But here's the most terrifying part - it's not just a remote possibility, it's a looming probability in our current state of SaaS security.

But the nightmare doesn't end there. It escalates. Imagine our emergency services – police, fire departments, and EMTs, who are rapidly digitizing their operations, being suddenly impeded. A SaaS data breach could disrupt the real-time flow of vital information that these services rely on to save lives. Think of a 911 dispatcher unable to locate an emergency caller due to a system failure. In such scenarios, the cost is human lives.

Our civic systems, from traffic lights to waste management, increasingly rely on SaaS platforms. A disruption in these systems could plunge cities into disorder, compromising public safety and bringing daily life to a standstill.

And if we dare to extrapolate, we reach a point of existential threat - our national security. In this digital era, our adversaries don't need to declare a traditional war; they merely need to compromise our digital defenses. Imagine a future where our nuclear arsenal, potentially controlled through SaaS applications, is at risk.

These scenarios are indeed alarming. They're meant to be. They serve to underline the fact that SaaS data apocalypse isn't a confined business problem, it's a societal threat. The cost of inaction is not just monetary loss, but potential endangerment of lives and the very way we live.

Our defenseless, our vulnerable, those we have a duty to protect, are at risk. This is the heart-wrenching, terrifying reality we confront as we peer into the abyss of a full-blown SaaS data apocalypse. But as much as this reality may frighten us, it should also spur us into action. The future is not yet written, and it's in our hands to ensure that these worst-case scenarios remain within the realm of imagination. The key to that future lies in acknowledging the threat, understanding its implications, and then acting decisively to safeguard our world.

The Y2K Nightmare Realized

The Y2K scare of the millennium's turn, despite the hype and hysteria, fizzled out to be little more than an infamous blip in the annals of computing history. We all held our collective breath as the clock ticked over into the 21st century, waiting for the widely prophesied digital Armageddon. It was supposed to be a catastrophe, a doomsday event birthed from the simplicity of a two-digit line of code that had failed to account for the year 2000.

Anticipations ranged from the mildly disruptive to the downright apocalyptic. Planes were to plummet from the sky, hurtling into a world now uncharted by malfunctioning GPS systems. Traffic lights, suddenly robbed of their temporal awareness, were supposed to malfunction, causing gridlocks, accidents, and chaos. Banks were expected to collapse, their databases failing to recognize the new millennium. And thus, we were told, our world would descend into an unparalleled chaos because of this 'millennium bug'.

But as we all know, that didn't happen. The year 2000 arrived with the usual fanfare and festivities, but without the expected technological catastrophe. The world kept spinning, planes kept flying, traffic lights kept changing, and banks carried on with their business. The doomsday scenario was averted, not by divine intervention, but by the diligent work of programmers worldwide who had toiled to fix the coding errors and update the systems.

Fast forward twenty-three years to 2023, and the specter of the Y2K bug seems a quaint memory. Yet, in a cruel twist of irony, we find ourselves living in the world that the Y2K scare had predicted, but for reasons wholly unanticipated. The nightmares of Y2K, which we evaded in 2000, are coming to life, not due to a benign coding oversight, but due to a malicious and insidious threat – ransomware, spurred by SaaS data breaches.

We now exist in a world where a simple ransomware attack could potentially have the devastating impact, we feared Y2K would. Our dependence on SaaS applications has created a precarious digital landscape. SaaS data breaches have the potential to disrupt our society's very fabric, akin to the Y2K scare, but with a higher probability of becoming a reality.

In this uncanny reality, systems critical to our society's functioning—traffic control systems, hospital databases, even our nuclear arsenal—could be crippled by ransomware attacks. The chaos we feared in Y2K could manifest in an even grimmer reality today, not because of a coding oversight but due to deliberate, malicious actions. The impact, much like the anticipated Y2K disaster, could be monumental. But unlike the Y2K scare, the threats we face today are not potential—they're imminent.

Thus, the nightmare of Y2K is now our reality. We live in a world where the specter of societal collapse due to technological failure is not merely a hypothetical scenario but a tangible threat. But unlike Y2K, this threat isn't due to a simple coding error—it's a far more malicious beast. SaaS data breaches have brought us to the precipice of the very chaos we feared two decades ago. The difference is, this time, the threat is real, it's immediate, and we must act to prevent our worst fears from coming true.

The Financial Sector: A Perfect Target

As we delve deeper into the dystopian realms of SaaS data breaches, there's an industry that inevitably surfaces as a primary concern: the financial services sector. This realm, which literally and figuratively underpins the economic fabric of our society, represents an almost irresistible target for cybercriminals. Let's paint a vivid picture of what the worst-case scenario could look like for this sector, which impacts everyone, from the smallest savers to the largest corporations.

The shift towards digitization within the financial sector has been remarkable. Major players, like Goldman Sachs, are even declaring themselves as technology companies as much as they are traditional financial institutions. The wheels of finance are increasingly driven by algorithms, and the brick-and-mortar bank is giving way to online platforms and mobile applications. There is an incalculable value attached to these digital assets, and this value is a blazing beacon that attracts cybercriminals like moths to a flame.

One can hardly exaggerate the importance of the digital assets now controlled by these financial institutions. Among the most valuable are the codebases stored on SaaS platforms, intricate digital blueprints that contain the DNA of the banking world. These codebases are the pulse of the financial world, guiding transactions, main-

taining security, enabling communication, and support-
ing the decision-making that shapes our economy. In
other words, the digital assets of these institutions aren't
just valuable – they're the lifeblood of our economic system.

The potential impact of these digital assets being compromised doesn't bear thinking about. The consequences
could range from the severely disruptive to the outright
catastrophic. In the worst-case scenario, the very foundation of our economy could be shaken. Attackers, once
in possession of these digital keys to the financial king-
dom, could potentially hold these institutions hostage
for astronomical sums, plunging the world into a financial crisis the likes of which we've never seen.

It's a chilling prospect – financial institutions having to
negotiate with cybercriminals for the release of their
own assets, with billions, possibly trillions of dollars, and
the stability of global economies hanging in the balance.
The fallout would not be limited to the financial sector
alone. It could lead to the collapse of global stock markets, currency crashes, or even economic depression,
affecting not only corporations but also individuals.

In summary, as the financial sector increasingly moves
towards digitization, the stakes become exponentially
higher. With each line of code written, with each piece of
data stored on SaaS platforms, the value of digital assets

surges, but so does the vulnerability. The potential impact of a major breach could result in a catastrophic financial crisis that could ripple through the entire global economy. This is a terrifying prospect, highlighting the urgent need for proactive steps to secure our digital future.

Real World Examples: The Reality of SaaS Data Breaches

The realities of SaaS data breaches are far from hypothetical; we have already seen disturbingly concrete examples. These real-world instances demonstrate how devastating such attacks can be, illuminating the tangible threats and palpable consequences we face.

The SolarWinds hack, for instance, stands as a stark example of the possible devastation. It was one of the most sophisticated and pervasive cyberattacks in history, infiltrating the systems of thousands of companies and government organizations across the globe. This attack was a chilling demonstration of how even the most secure networks could be compromised, resulting in the exposure of sensitive data on an unprecedented scale (Solar Winds Attack, 2023).

However, the problem doesn't stop at the attacks themselves. A pressing issue within the industry is the persistent lack of transparency about such attacks. The reluctance or failure to disclose breaches not only leaves consumers and stakeholders in the dark but also means that organizations don't learn from each other's experiences. This lack of information exchange impedes the development of robust defense mechanisms, effectively leaving every entity to fend for themselves in an increasingly hostile digital environment.

To delve deeper into the effects of these breaches, let's consider the instance of CNA Financial (CNA Paid $40 Million to Ransom, 2019). This company fell prey to a crippling ransomware attack that resulted in significant repercussions. The attack didn't just compromise the company's operational efficiency, but also shook its reputation, shaking the trust of customers and stakeholders alike.

However, the vulnerabilities are not restricted to sectors like finance. The healthcare industry, one of the most regulated and seemingly protected industries, has also witnessed its share of attacks. The WannaCry ransomware attack in 2017 (Factsheet, Wannacry, 2018), for instance, crippled the UK's National Health Service, causing widespread disruption. In this attack, the perpetrators didn't just aim for a financial payout; they sought to cripple a critical public service, demonstrating that cyber threats have the potential to inflict real-world harm and chaos.

In another example, the US-based health insurance provider, Anthem, fell victim to one of the largest data breaches in history in 2015, with nearly 78.8 million people's records exposed (Anthem Security Breach, 2015). This instance underlined that even companies tasked with safeguarding sensitive personal data are vulnerable to such breaches, causing a ripple effect of fear and uncertainty among the populace.

The energy sector hasn't been immune either. The Colonial Pipeline, the largest fuel pipeline in the United States, was the victim of a ransomware attack in May 2021. The attack infected some of the pipeline's digital systems, shutting it down for several days. The attack caused gas shortages, price surges, and consumer panic (Colonial Pipeline Shuts, 2021). The event underscored the immense societal disruption that could be caused by such breaches, taking the threat from the digital sphere into the physical world.

These real-world examples serve as a wake-up call. They underline the urgent need for an industry-wide shift in mindset and strategy. We are not dealing with hypothetical scenarios or distant threats. We are wrestling with real, present dangers. The SaaS data apocalypse is not just a looming horizon; it's already upon us. Hence, the call to action is clear: there is an immediate need for comprehensive security measures and greater transparency in the industry. The consequences of inaction are simply too dire to contemplate.

Conclusion: Facing the SaaS Data Apocalypse

The unfolding of the SaaS data apocalypse is a harsh reality we cannot ignore. It's not just a hypothetical doomsday scenario confined to the realm of science fiction. It's our current reality, a nightmare that's unfolding around us with every passing day, threatening to plunge us into a world where chaos reigns and vulnerabilities are exploited on an unimaginable scale.

From children in schools to the patient on the operating table, from emergency services to national security, from our financial institutions to every sector of industry that relies on SaaS platforms for their operation, everyone is at risk. The repercussions of these breaches have already been felt, causing severe economic, social, and even human harm. This narrative is no longer about isolated incidents, but about a systematic failure that affects us all on a global scale.

However, amid the disquiet and doom, we must remember that every crisis also presents an opportunity. It beckons us to innovate, to redefine the norms, and to catalyze a significant shift. It's important to remember that the very fabric of humanity is woven with resilience and ingenuity. Just as we have grappled with and overcome countless adversities in the past, we can, and must, rise to this occasion.

The gravity of the SaaS data apocalypse, while alarming, also provides a unique impetus for innovation. This challenge requires groundbreaking solutions that not only safeguard against the immediate threats but also fortify us against the unknown risks of the future. It's not merely about securing our present but also about ensuring a safer, more secure digital tomorrow.

The call to action is clear. We need to move beyond traditional approaches to cybersecurity. We need to develop new methodologies, technologies, and policies that ensure the secure storage and use of data in the SaaS landscape. It is an immense task, but one that is not beyond our collective capability.

In the upcoming chapter, we will begin this exciting and vital journey. I will lay out the initial groundwork for these much-needed solutions. We will explore innovative strategies and breakthrough solutions that can mitigate the risks and ensure the safe use of SaaS platforms. We will look at how we can infuse transparency, accountability, and security into every layer of our digital interactions, whether it's in the financial sector, healthcare, education, or any other industry that relies on these platforms.

This is more than just a quest for solutions. It's a call for a collective awakening. A plea for collaborative action.

A challenge that tests our resilience, creativity, and our unwavering commitment to safeguard our digital world.

In conclusion, the SaaS data apocalypse is indeed a daunting reality, a storm that's already upon us. But let's remember that it's the harshest of storms that yield the most beautiful rainbows. And as we confront this challenge, I'm confident that we will witness an outpouring of innovative solutions that will not only weather this storm but also usher in a safer, stronger, and more secure digital age.

Are you prepared to recover from a ransomware attack?

Scan this QR code to find out what your R-Score is today!

CHAPTER 4

The Invisible Apocalypse: Shattering SaaS Data Protection Myths

In today's era of digital transformation, SaaS, has emerged as a beacon of efficiency, streamlining, and innovation. This model has democratized access to powerful tools, opening up avenues for businesses to operate with unprecedented agility and speed. Yet, beneath this veneer of convenience, a storm is brewing. This storm - the SaaS data apocalypse, as I call it - is looming on the horizon, a threat that remains largely invisible to many until it is too late.

Data has unequivocally become the lifeblood of organizations. It's the raw material powering insights, decisions, and strategies that are the heartbeat of modern business. But in the switch to SaaS platforms, companies are often unknowingly throwing their data into an abyss, leaving it open to a new breed of threats that were previously unheard of. Data, that once sat under lock and key in on-premises servers, now resides in the vast expanse of the cloud - a blessing and a curse.

The rise of SaaS has in many ways opened Pandora's box, multiplying the potential entry points for cybercriminals, and exponentially increasing the risk surface area. As a result, organizations are fighting a constant battle against unseen foes, safeguarding their data treasure troves from being infiltrated or held hostage.

Yet, the gravity of the situation often does not hit home until disaster strikes. People don't think about this stuff seriously until shit happens. Indeed, just like a natural disaster or a health pandemic, the scale and the impact of the problem do not become real until we are caught in its epicenter. This delayed reaction, however, comes at a grave cost.

This chapter is designed to unravel the complex fabric of the invisible SaaS data apocalypse, making the unseen seen. It is not intended to instill fear, but to illuminate the truth of our current reality. We will explore the landscape of this crisis, examining its impact on different communities within the business ecosystem, and most importantly, discussing strategies to tackle this head-on.

In this exploration, we will come across narratives that might seem unsettling, perhaps even overwhelming. But remember, forewarned is forearmed. The more we understand the depth and breadth of this challenge, the better equipped we are to face it.

As CEO of HYCU, a company at the forefront of tackling this data protection crisis, I've been at the epicenter of these seismic shifts, witnessing firsthand the struggles of businesses and the critical need for robust data protection strategies. The goal is to distill these experiences, observations, and insights into a resource that empowers you to navigate this crisis with confidence.

Through the course of this chapter, we will delve into the communities bound by this common challenge, the transformation of the data protection industry, the specific dilemmas that SaaS data security poses, and how we can approach a solution. As we journey into the belly of the beast, let's bear in mind that while the threat is formidable, it's not insurmountable. After all, it's in the face of adversity that we often find our greatest strengths and innovations.

Affected Communities: Shared Concerns, Shared Interests

As the SaaS data apocalypse draws closer, various communities within the business world are increasingly finding themselves bound by shared interests and concerns, all revolving around data security. The issue, once dismissed as an arcane concern relegated to the backrooms of the IT department, has now stepped into the spotlight, becoming a priority for key stakeholders at every level of organizational hierarchy.

CISOs, CIOs, and Chief Risk Officers: The Digital Gatekeepers

At the forefront of this unfolding crisis are the CISOs (Chief Information Security Officers), CIOs (Chief Information Officers), and Chief Risk Officers (CROs). These executives form the bedrock of an organization's cybersecurity defense, tasked with the responsibility of protecting the company's digital assets, including its most vital component - data.

In the era of SaaS, their roles have evolved from maintaining the integrity of on-premises systems to navigating a far more complex, multifaceted terrain. It's not merely about guarding against the potential incursion of external threats anymore. It's also about grappling with the intrinsic vulnerabilities that come with having data dispersed across a plethora of SaaS platforms.

These digital gatekeepers are consistently trying to strike a delicate balance - on one hand, enabling the organization to harness the power of SaaS, and on the other, ensuring this does not expose the company to an inordinate level of risk. As the threat landscape continues to evolve at a breakneck pace, they find themselves in an unending race against time, constantly learning, adapting, and preparing for worst-case scenarios.

Boards of Directors: A New Item on the Agenda

With the stakes higher than ever, data security and data protection are making their way up the corporate ladder, capturing the attention of Boards of Directors. Previously untouched by the nitty-gritty of cybersecurity, board members are now being urged to take active interest in the state of their organization's data protection measures.

They are starting to hear from their lawyers that, "Hey, if you haven't taken precautions, a time will come when you're going to be responsible." It's becoming clear that ignorance or a lack of understanding is no longer a valid excuse. In an era where data breaches could potentially wipe out a company's reputation and bottom line, the Board's responsibility extends to ensuring the company is cyber-resilient, has a solid business continuity plan, and a robust data backup system in place.

CEOs: A Growing Fear

CEOs, often revered for their strength and foresight, are beginning to feel the heat. Fear is creeping in - fear of becoming the next victim of a catastrophic data breach, and the resulting damage it can do to their leadership and the company at large.

As the leader of the organization, CEOs are responsible for setting the strategic direction and tone for the entire company, including its approach to data security. They need to ensure that cybersecurity is not just about prevention and detection, but also about remediation - the ability to recover swiftly and efficiently in the event of a breach.

In a nutshell, it's a wake-up call for the business world. From CISOs to CEOs, everyone is reckoning with the SaaS data apocalypse. It's forcing a rethink of traditional security strategies and pushing organizations towards creating a more robust, resilient defense against the rapidly evolving threat landscape.

The SaaS Data Security Dilemma

The emergence of SaaS has undoubtedly revolutionized business operations worldwide. It's like the digital equivalent of Mary Poppins' magic bag - bringing forth a tool for every business need, all with the comfort of user-friendly, game-like interfaces. But beneath this surface-level simplicity lies a complex labyrinth of data security challenges. The SaaS universe, for all its benefits, has birthed a set of critical issues that collectively constitute a formidable data security dilemma.

Data Silos and Sprawl: The Disintegration of Unity

The digital era has presented us with a bounty of tools and platforms, most notably SaaS applications, designed to improve our productivity, streamline operations, and foster collaboration. These advancements, as transformative as they are, come with an ironic downside. The more we fragment our data across different platforms, the more vulnerable we become. This dispersal of data makes us an enticing target for ransomware attackers. Their logic is simple, akin to a bandit choosing to rob multiple vulnerable homes over a single fortified castle.

Unlike traditional on-premises infrastructures, SaaS platforms result in data being scattered across a multitude of online services, each operating in its own self-contained environment. Imagine your data as a flock of sheep; now, instead of being safely corralled within a single pen, they're roaming free across a vast open field.

To truly understand the scale of the issue, we have to delve into some sobering statistics. Over 52% of companies have already fallen victim to a SaaS-related ransomware event. The exponential growth of SaaS applications in recent years has made this landscape even more enticing for cybercriminals. These platforms, designed for ease of use and scalability, often prioritize user experience over stringent security measures, at least in their out-of-the-box configurations.

This scattering of data makes visualization and protection significantly more challenging. Without a comprehensive, bird's eye view of where all your data resides, how can you even begin to protect it? Every new SaaS platform added to the ecosystem increases the sprawl, further complicating the task of data security. It's like trying to herd cats - a virtually impossible task without the right tools and strategies in place.

User Adoption: An Overlooked Security Vulnerability

Traditionally, the purchase and integration of new software was the domain of IT departments. Their expertise ensured that any new addition met the company's security and integration standards. But today, in the SaaS-dominated world, this central authority is often bypassed. Department heads from sales to marketing, armed with credit cards and the promise of productivity enhancements, can rapidly onboard new tools. It's an era where software buying isn't restricted; it's proliferated. It's as if everyone's a software buyer, impulsively adding to the shopping cart without fully considering the security implications.

The attraction of SaaS platforms lies in their promise of instant solutions to pressing problems. A sales team struggling with client relationship management can swiftly integrate a new CRM tool. A marketing team needing analytics can almost instantaneously get their hands on a new data visualization tool. The problem? This impulse buying often happens without the necessary due diligence on the software's security credentials.

For many department leads, the main criterion for a new tool is its functionality. Does it do the job? Is it user-friendly? Will it drive results? Often, the question of security takes a backseat. As a result, sensitive data might be dumped into platforms that haven't been vetted for robust security features.

This is where the analogy of the homeowner comes into play. Just as handing out house keys without thorough scrutiny can lead to break-ins, hastily importing data into unverified SaaS tools is an open invitation to cyberattacks.

A breach in one department's tool can have cascading effects across the entire organization. Consider, for instance, a CRM tool that gets compromised. Suddenly, cybercriminals might have access to a treasure trove of customer data, from email addresses to purchase histories. The implications? Phishing attacks, financial fraud, and a tarnished brand reputation, to name a few.

Unsanctioned user adoption is one of the most pressing concerns for companies navigating the intricate world of SaaS. While it's tempting to place stringent controls or impose top-down decisions, doing so might stifle the innovative spirit of departments. A more nuanced approach requires nurturing a culture of security awareness that empowers teams while also safeguarding the organization's digital assets.

The Strategy to Counter Unsanctioned User Adoption

In today's intricate world of SaaS, unsanctioned user adoption has emerged as a major concern for many organizations. While the easy route might be to instate strict controls or enforce decisions from the top, doing so could stifle the innovative drive inherent within different departments. A more balanced approach lies in nurturing a culture of security awareness, where teams feel both empowered and responsible.

Education is pivotal in this culture shift. It goes beyond a mere checklist of dos and don'ts. Teams must grasp the essence of "why" behind these guidelines. Introducing them to real-world case studies of companies that have suffered breaches due to unsanctioned tools can underscore the importance of cautious software adoption. As security threats are ever evolving, it's equally crucial to provide regular training sessions, possibly on a quarterly basis. And instead of traditional, lecture-style training, hands-on workshops, simulations, and interactive sessions can be more effective, making the training resonate more with employees.

Meanwhile, centralized vetting offers a pathway for teams to embrace new tools without compromising security. By establishing a knowledge base of pre-vetted tools, companies can guide departments towards safer choices. If a department stumbles upon a new tool that seems promising, it's imperative for the IT team to have a swift and efficient vetting system. Any delay might tempt teams to skip the official process. Transparency is key; once the assessment is over, the decision—whether it's an approval, conditional use, or a denial—should be clearly communicated, outlining the reasons behind it.

Lastly, open communication between the IT teams and departments is crucial. Periodic forums or meetings where departments can share their software needs can foster a collaborative spirit. By jointly exploring potential tools, the chosen solutions are more likely to meet both the functional requirements of the department and the security standards of the organization. Furthermore, by maintaining open channels for feedback on existing tools or processes, companies not only refine their tech stack but also cultivate a sense of ownership and involvement among their teams.

Managing the challenge of unsanctioned user adoption strikes a balance between granting autonomy and ensuring security. By emphasizing education, facilitating a vetting process, and promoting open dialogue, organizations can establish a harmonious environment where decision-making is both empowered and aligned with corporate security standards.

Vendor Responsibility: The Blurred Lines of Accountability

In recent years, as the cloud ecosystem has burgeoned, so has the complexity of the associated security challenges. One notable concern is the delineation of responsibility when it comes to data security in SaaS environments. A vendor's role and responsibility in this matrix have become a topic of great debate and, at times, confusion.

SaaS vendors often present themselves as bastions of security, exhibiting an array of impressive certifications and compliance emblems that can be likened to a medieval knight brandishing his gleaming armor in preparation for battle. Their marketing materials resound with assurances of robust security measures designed to keep breaches at bay. However, it's worth noting that while these security protocols are impressive, they are by no means absolute guarantees against cyber threats.

When pressed about the specifics of data protection, many vendors showcase an adeptness in circumventing the subject. While their platforms might be built to be as impenetrable as possible, they can sometimes display a hesitancy in shouldering the overarching responsibility of data security. This subtle deflection is not just a sign of vendors trying to limit their liability; it's an acknowledgment of a more profound truth: that while a SaaS platform can be made resilient against threats, the onus of protecting the data within often falls on the shoulders of its owner.

This reality leads to a nuanced dance between vendors and customers. Businesses, especially those less familiar with the intricacies of cloud security, might be lulled into a false sense of security by the shiny badges and assurances presented by SaaS vendors. They might misconstrue platform security for total data protection. Such an assumption can have dire consequences. It is therefore paramount for organizations to delineate and understand the shared responsibility model. While vendors maintain the security of the platform, users must ensure their data's safety and integrity by employing best practices, appropriate access controls, and regular audits.

In tackling the complex conundrum of SaaS data security, businesses need to be proactive, discerning, and comprehensive in their approach. It isn't just about ensuring that vendors have adequate measures in place; it's also about understanding the vulnerabilities inherent in one's own operations and addressing them robustly. To mitigate risks, businesses need to evolve, ensuring that their data protection strategies are holistic and adaptive.

The Shared Responsibility Model in SaaS Data Security

In the complex ecosystem of SaaS data security, the shared responsibility model stands as a beacon, guiding both SaaS providers and users towards a collaborative defense mechanism. This model delineates the boundaries of duty; while the provider is responsible for the security of the underlying infrastructure, from physical servers to foundational software, the customer shoulders the responsibility of data management, user access control, and fine-tuning application-specific security settings. Essentially, the vendor provides a secure platform, but it's up to the customer to leverage it securely. It's a synergy where both parties are inextricably linked, underscoring that robust SaaS data security isn't just about the vendor or user in isolation but a joint venture of both.

However, this harmonious picture of shared duty isn't without its wrinkles. The very premise of the model, which expects a clear understanding of roles by both the SaaS providers and their customers, often crumbles in the face of misunderstandings and ambiguities. There's a prevalent misconception among users that vendors, with their array of security badges and certifications, provide an all-encompassing security net. This fallacy can lead to complacency, where businesses neglect essential security measures on their end. This oversight is further exacerbated by the modern tech stack's complexity, with each integrated SaaS tool bringing its own set of security challenges. Unsolicited and unchecked adoption of SaaS tools by departments, without adequate security vetting, introduces additional vulnerabilities. Moreover, not all vendors are created equal.

Some, especially newcomers or smaller entities, may lack the comprehensive security infrastructure found in more established providers. An over-reliance on certifications can also mislead, as these badges, while indicative of standards, don't vouch for impenetrable security. The ever-evolving digital threat landscape adds another layer of complexity, making static responsibility divisions potentially harmful. Lastly, the model's efficacy hinges on open, continuous communication between providers and users, which, when lacking, can leave significant security blind spots.

The world of SaaS security is akin to a multifaceted gem, with each facet representing a unique challenge. Its complexity is undeniable, and the associated stakes monumental. In this landscape, complacency is a luxury no business can afford. As the weight of responsibility mounts, businesses must rise to the occasion, comprehending the nuances of this challenge and strategizing accordingly. The solution to the SaaS security puzzle lies not in isolating the challenges but in understanding and integrating them. The future, and the security of invaluable data, depends on it.

Navigating the Unseen Apocalypse

In the contemporary world of SaaS, we have come face to face with an invisible yet relentless enemy: the threats to our valuable data. This chapter presented an incisive look into this burgeoning crisis and its implications for businesses globally. The virtual landscape, once a promised land of limitless potential, has now become a battleground teeming with unseen adversaries.

We delved into the affected communities grappling with the urgency of data protection, from the top tier executives such as CISOs, CIOs, and Chief Risk Officers to the boards of directors and CEOs. All are increasingly recognizing their shared responsibility and potential liability in the face of significant data breaches. This chapter brought to light the critical dilemmas surrounding SaaS data security. We examined the unique challenges posed by data silos and sprawl, the often-unconsidered security implications associated with user adoption of SaaS tools, and the shifting responsibilities of vendors in assuring data security. However, amidst these trials, we charted a path forward.

With platforms like HYCU at our disposal, we have the tools to safeguard our data kingdoms. Looking ahead, it's essential to acknowledge that while we've laid the foundation for effective SaaS data protection, our journey is far from over. It's not enough to build our fortresses; we need to scrutinize our perceptions about this monumental problem and challenge the prevailing assumptions. In the next chapter, we will delve deeper into these perceptions.

We'll examine some of the prevailing myths about SaaS data security and uncover the truth beneath them. It's time to question the conventional wisdom, deconstruct the misinformation, and establish an enlightened understanding of our data landscapes. Real-world solutions are not born out of hastily drawn plans; they emerge from a thorough understanding of the problem at hand, extensive research, collaboration, and iterative refinement.

Scan this QR Code to find out what SaaS data you may have unprotected with R-Graph.

CHAPTER 5

Perceptions and Assumptions: SaaS Data Protection Myths

As the CEO of HYCU, a company deeply immersed in the SaaS landscape, I've had countless conversations with organizations of various sizes, from startups to multinational corporations. These interactions have revealed a troubling reality: businesses often operate under several misconceptions about SaaS data protection, and this misaligned understanding poses a significant risk to their data integrity and security.

To make meaningful changes, we must first address these misguided beliefs. These perceptions – while they may seem innocuous or even logical at first glance – often result in practices that leave companies vulnerable. By challenging and reshaping these perceptions, we can guide businesses towards more effective and secure strategies, thereby enhancing our collective approach to SaaS data protection.

This chapter is centered around five common perceptions about SaaS, which I've frequently encountered in my professional journey. These include the belief that an organization doesn't rely heavily on SaaS, the assumption that all SaaS and cloud data are protected by the vendor, the misconception that current backup vendors sufficiently protect SaaS data, the false sense of security against ransomware attacks, and the mistaken equivalence of Single Sign-On (SSO) with comprehensive data protection.

We'll scrutinize each perception, discuss why it's erroneous, and present counter-arguments grounded in facts and statistics. I'll share insights from industry research, our experiences at HYCU, and the lessons we've learned along the way. In doing so, we aim to reveal the true picture of SaaS data protection, one that necessitates greater understanding, heightened vigilance, and the adoption of specialized solutions.

Our goal here is not merely to point out the fallacies but to lay the groundwork for effective solutions. By acknowledging and comprehending these misconceptions, organizations can prepare themselves to better navigate the ever-evolving SaaS landscape. This understanding marks the first crucial step towards robust data protection – a step that is imperative in today's interconnected digital world.

Join me as we uncover the truth behind these prevalent perceptions, understand their implications, and chart a path forward. This journey is not just about reframing the narrative around SaaS data protection. It's about empowering organizations to regain control over their data, reinforcing trust in their SaaS investments, and ultimately, securing their digital future. The journey towards better SaaS data protection begins here.

Perception: "Our Organization Doesn't Rely Heavily on SaaS"

One of the main misconceptions that we see out there today, and this is of organizations of all sizes, is this idea that your organization does not rely heavily on SaaS.

Many CIOs and IT departments think contextually about their own business. They think about what they're looking at each and every day, and that may very well not be SaaS. But then, if you ask a follow-up question and say, "Are you really telling me that nobody in your marketing department has signed up for a SaaS service in the last year? Nobody in your sales department, no one in your engineering department, no one in your manufacturing department?" All of a sudden, you see the wheels start to spin.

Many businesses, from small enterprises to multinational corporations, operate under the assumption that they don't rely heavily on SaaS. In my experience as the

CEO of HYCU, this is far from the truth. A number of times, I've seen a company estimate a small number of SaaS applications in use, only to be astounded when the actual count is much higher.

For example, when we conducted an internal audit at HYCU, we estimated we were using around 12 SaaS services. The actual number? A staggering 75. Despite our own role in the SaaS industry, we had underestimated our reliance on these services. It underlines a critical point: many businesses simply don't comprehend the extent to which they rely on others' software and services, and how that lack of control can impact them.

This perception isn't exclusive to us. According to research by Okta, a leading identity and access management provider, the average mid-market company uses a whopping 217 SaaS applications and databases (Key Findings SaaS Management, 2022). That's an astounding number, and it showcases how pervasive and integral SaaS has become to modern business operations.

Indeed, the reality of our time is that SaaS has become the backbone of modern businesses. The ease of deployment, the scalability, the reduction in capital expenditure, and the potential for seamless collaboration - all these factors have contributed to the pervasive use of SaaS in enterprises worldwide. However, this widespread adoption often goes unnoticed, or is grossly underestimated, largely due to the lack of visibility and oversight.

When we talk about our experience at HYCU, it wasn't that we intentionally ignored our SaaS usage. We are, after all, a SaaS company ourselves. However, because SaaS solutions are typically easy to deploy and manage, and often require little more than an internet connection and a credit card to get started, many teams within our organization independently adopted various tools to streamline their work. This happened without necessarily going through a centralized IT approval process, leading to a situation we often refer to as 'Shadow IT.'

'Shadow IT' refers to the IT systems or solutions used within a company without the knowledge or approval of the corporate IT department. This phenomenon is not unique to HYCU. In fact, according to a survey by Cisco, up to 80% of employees admit to using non-approved SaaS applications in their jobs. This stark number shows that despite IT's best efforts, the use of SaaS applications can, and often does, run rampant within an organization.

This rise in Shadow IT is fueled by the 'consumerization' of IT, where user-friendly, over-the-counter SaaS applications meet the specific needs of teams better than the organization's standard, often more cumbersome, software. Unfortunately, this decentralized decision-making can lead to security vulnerabilities and other risks.

Consider this scenario: a marketing team within a company decides to use a new SaaS-based email marketing tool. They find it user-friendly and well-suited to their needs. However, they neglect to consider the implications of storing customer data, possibly including sensitive information, on this new platform. Without appropriate IT oversight and data protection measures in place, the company could be exposed to significant security and compliance risks.

When we discovered our 'Shadow IT' at HYCU, it served as a wake-up call. It wasn't about policing our teams or restricting the use of effective tools, but about understanding and acknowledging our reliance on these services. We took measures to ensure that all our SaaS solutions were secure, compliant, and that we had appropriate data protection measures in place.

The Okta research mentioned above is further evidence of the underestimation of SaaS usage. This research shows the vast numbers of SaaS applications being used in organizations of all sizes. However, this is not a call for panic but an invitation for awareness, understanding, and action. Recognizing the prevalence of SaaS in your organization is the first step in effectively managing and securing it.

The perception that "We don't use much SaaS in our organization" is often incorrect. SaaS has become integral to modern businesses, and it's important for organizations to recognize and appropriately manage their usage. This starts with an accurate inventory of all SaaS applications in use, followed by implementing comprehensive governance, risk management, and data protection strategies to secure the organization's digital assets.

Perception: "My SaaS and cloud data are protected by the vendor"

The notion that SaaS vendors or cloud providers are responsible for the complete protection of user data is a popular, albeit potentially damaging, misconception. The vast majority of SaaS providers follow a shared responsibility model, implying that while they are responsible for infrastructure, application uptime, and certain security measures, they do not shoulder full responsibility for user data protection.

For instance, consider the high-profile cases of Microsoft 365 and Salesforce. Both are globally recognized SaaS giants and understandably inspire a great deal of trust in their clientele. But a thorough examination of their respective service agreements reveals interesting clauses. Although these vendors provide robust backup infrastructure for their own use (e.g., server failure, disaster recovery), they explicitly state that they aren't responsible for data loss caused by user actions. Any accidental or intentional deletions, corruptions, or modifications of data by users are essentially the users' responsibility.

I would challenge any of you to reach out to your top ten SaaS vendors, send them an email, and say you deleted all the data from their SaaS application on a particular day, and you want all that day's data back within the next 24 hours. The harsh reality is that only one out of those top ten or 20 will have the internal capabilities to recover your data quickly and in a usable format.

Backing up data is the easy part, but the ability to recover that data in a usable format, not a big giant CSV file, is what's going to make it valuable to you and allow true resiliency and business continuity in your business.

One of the best ways to understand why SaaS vendors aren't protecting your data is to examine the shared responsibility model. This model essentially says that SaaS vendors will allow you to leverage their platform, but you have the responsibility for your own data. Unfortunately, the shared responsibility model is often buried in contracts, but it is there somewhere in the terms and conditions.

A Real-World Example: Microsoft Office 365

If you need further evidence, examine the Microsoft Office 365 Services Agreement. In recent years, they've had to move all the stipulations around data protection, data management, and shared responsibility from page fourteen to page one of the terms and conditions. This change occurred because so many people believed their data was protected, and when they found out it was not, it became a real problem.

This is not a lack of intent by SaaS vendors. A well-known billion-dollar ARR SaaS vendor recognized this problem and reached out to major enterprise data protection vendors. Every single one of them said that they didn't have the total addressable market to support building that protection, leaving the vendor with no option but to offer their customers no data protection.

The misunderstanding largely stems from the convenience offered by the SaaS model, leading some businesses to adopt a somewhat complacent attitude towards data security. The seamless access, simple user interface, and prompt technical assistance that characterize SaaS offerings can create an illusion of absolute safety. Yet, beneath this facade of security, the complexities of data ownership, responsibility, and protection persist.

Data protection should be viewed as a two-pronged process: prevention and recovery. While SaaS vendors excel at prevention—securing their infrastructure, regularly updating their software, and managing authentication—they don't always excel at recovery. Data recovery in the event of user error, malicious deletion, or even rogue applications often falls on the shoulders of the customers.

Moreover, different regulations worldwide, such as the European General Data Protection Regulation (GDPR) or the California Consumer Privacy Act (CCPA), place the onus of personal data protection squarely on businesses. Therefore, regardless of where the data is stored or processed, it's the responsibility of the business to ensure the appropriate safeguards are in place.

So, how can businesses better protect themselves? A crucial starting point is to understand their responsibility towards their data. Thoroughly reviewing service agreements and understanding the terms of service can help. These agreements may seem like complex, legal jargon, but they outline the scope and limitations of a vendor's responsibility towards data protection.

Implementing a robust, independent backup and recovery solution is another proactive measure businesses can take. Such solutions can safeguard against data loss from accidental deletion, security threats, or even service outages. Furthermore, regular audits and risk assessments can help identify vulnerabilities and gaps in data protection strategies.

In the world of SaaS, where data is the new oil, organizations need to dispel the myth that their data is entirely protected by their vendors. Data protection is a shared responsibility—one that requires vigilance, proactive measures, and a clear understanding of the scope and limits of vendor responsibility.

Perception: "My current backup vendor already protects my SaaS data"

A prevalent perception among businesses is the assumption that their existing backup solution provides adequate protection for their SaaS data. This belief is often fueled by the assumption that backup solutions are universally adaptable to any type of data, including those hosted on SaaS platforms. However, as we delve deeper into this issue, we will see why this perception is not just erroneous but potentially dangerous.

According to Gartner, a leading industry analyst firm that tracks the enterprise backup and recovery market, of the 23,000 vendors offering backup solutions, less than five provide specific services for SaaS data protection (Gartner Magic Quadrant for Enterprise Backup and Recovery Software Solutions, 2023). This statistic is astonishing and emphasizes the growing disconnect between the rapid adoption of SaaS applications and the lagging implementation of appropriate data protection measures.

The underlying reason behind this discrepancy lies in the unique nature of SaaS data. Traditional backup solutions were designed with on-premises data in mind. These solutions are effective for protecting data on local servers and hardware. However, the architecture and design of SaaS platforms are fundamentally different from traditional on-premises setups, resulting in distinct challenges for data protection.

Firstly, SaaS applications typically store data in the cloud, distributed across multiple servers in different geographical locations. This distribution enhances accessibility and reliability but complicates data protection efforts. Traditional backup solutions aren't designed to handle this level of complexity and may fail to fully capture or restore the entirety of the SaaS data.

Secondly, the dynamic nature of SaaS data, frequently updated and altered, presents additional challenges. Traditional backup solutions may not be capable of performing real-time or frequent enough backups to capture these changes, resulting in outdated backups and potential data loss.

Finally, SaaS platforms often use proprietary APIs for data interaction, making it difficult for traditional backup solutions to seamlessly integrate and interact with the data. This hurdle could result in incomplete backups, leading to potential data loss during recovery.

The above challenges emphasize the need for a specialized approach to SaaS data protection. Organizations must choose a solution that is specifically designed to handle the unique nature and challenges associated with SaaS data. These solutions should offer features such as real-time backup, direct integration with the SaaS platform's APIs, and the ability to manage distributed data across multiple locations.

Remember, assuming that traditional backup solutions protect your SaaS data is akin to assuming that a bicycle helmet will protect you in a car crash. While both are protective devices in their own right, they are designed for different scenarios and risks. Likewise, traditional backup solutions and SaaS data protection are distinct realms requiring different strategies and tools. In conclusion, it's essential for businesses to re-evaluate their backup strategies in light of their increasing reliance on SaaS platforms.

Perception: "We've made our organization ransomware proof"

The perception that an organization is immune to ransomware attacks, particularly concerning their SaaS applications, is a dangerous one. This complacency often arises from a misplaced faith in robust firewall configurations and the latest anti-malware solutions. Unfortunately, the reality of today's cybersecurity landscape tells a different, far grimmer story.

Odaseva, a renowned cybersecurity research firm, reports that more than half of all global companies have experienced a ransomware attack on their SaaS applications. (Odaseva, 2022). More alarming is the breach success rate of 52%. These statistics are not just figures on a report. They represent significant financial loss, damage to company reputation, and potential regulatory fines that impacted businesses have to deal with.

And this isn't just conjecture or fearmongering. Real-world examples abound. Garmin, a well-known GPS technology company, suffered a significant ransomware attack in July 2020 (BBC, 2020). This attack brought down several of its services, including those that customers depended on, like Garmin Connect, which tracks and analyzes health and fitness data. While Garmin never publicly confirmed it, reports suggest that they paid a multimillion-dollar ransom to recover their data.

In another instance, Blackbaud, a cloud software company serving the social good community, experienced a ransomware attack in May 2020 (Blackbaud to Pay $3 Million Over 'Erroneous' Breach Details, 2020). The attackers managed to exfiltrate a subset of data before Blackbaud's cybersecurity team could mitigate the attack. Despite paying the ransom and receiving assurances that the stolen data was destroyed, the breach had a substantial impact on Blackbaud's customers, who had to notify their stakeholders about the potential data compromise.

The point here isn't to inspire fear, but to impress upon organizations the urgent necessity for proactive and comprehensive SaaS data protection. It's not enough to react after an attack; prevention, detection, and quick response should be a business's guiding principles in today's digital age. This includes regularly updating and patching software, employing multi-factor authentication, training employees to recognize and avoid phishing attempts, and, importantly, implementing robust backup and recovery solutions for SaaS data.

Moreover, businesses need to understand that ransomware attacks are not just an IT problem; they have far-reaching consequences affecting all aspects of the organization. Hence, dealing with this threat requires a comprehensive, organization-wide approach, underpinned by the right blend of people, processes, and technology.

The perception of being "ransomware proof" needs a reality check. Businesses need to recognize the serious threat posed by ransomware attacks and take appropriate steps to safeguard their critical SaaS data, thus ensuring their resilience and business continuity in the face of potential cyber threats.

Perception: "Single Sign-On (SSO) for My SaaS Environment is All I Need"

Many organizations today are taking advantage of Single Sign-On (SSO) solutions. They do so with the understanding that SSO, which consolidates different application logins into a single login process, offers a powerful data protection capability. This perception, while true, when combined with an integrated data protection solution including one that can help visualize an entire data estate is a powerful combination.

SSO services are powerful solutions for convenience and to manage assets from a centralized place. They simplify the login process, improve the user experience, and mitigate the risk of password-related security breaches. The combination of SSO with the ability to visualize an entire date estate takes data protection to a new level. This is like securing your house with an advanced lock system and having all the doors and windows securely locked and safe from outside issues. When combined with integrated data protection, SSO can further protect against data loss arising from incidents like accidental deletions, malicious insiders, or even ransomware attacks.

Another strong positive, SSO when combined with integrated data protection can help to back up data and offer granular recovery options in the event of a data loss incident. For instance, if an employee mistakenly deletes a critical spreadsheet from a SaaS application, integrated data protection can help. Similarly, if a disgruntled employee intentionally destroys valuable data, integrated data protection can help recover that data. It's crucial to understand that SSO serves as a powerful gateway to your digital resources, and when combined with integrated data protection and the ability to visualize across the data estate to include SaaS applications, it can guarantee the safety of the data housed within the environment.

In this context, Okta, a forward-thinking and leading provider of SSO solutions, recognized the value in collaborating with data protection providers to provide the best jointly integrated solution possible. It's a major reason Okta Ventures invested in HYCU, a company specializing in multi-cloud data backup and recovery. This strategic move, in turn, helps extend Okta's strong value proposition to its customers, supplementing its top-tier access control capabilities with integrated data protection. This kind of joint offering demonstrates a keen understanding of the power that SSO with enhanced data protection can provide and enhance the SaaS data protection experience.

To illustrate the power of coupling SSO with a robust data backup solution, consider the case of a web-based DevOps lifecycle tool. Six years ago, an accidental deletion of a database resulted in significant data loss for the company. The company at the time was not using a tightly integrated data protection solution to help or aid in the restoration process. A solid data backup and recovery strategy could have helped mitigate the impacts of that disaster.

Understanding these five perceptions (and there are many others) and countering them with facts is of paramount importance to ensure the safety of an organization's SaaS data. By challenging these beliefs and providing concrete evidence to the contrary, we can influence the broader business community's approach to SaaS data protection. It is imperative to underscore the importance of adopting comprehensive and specialized data protection strategies, instead of relying on misconceptions and partial solutions. As the world increasingly relies on SaaS applications, we must take the necessary steps to secure our data in the cloud to ensure business continuity and the overall health of our organizations.

Perception is Reality.

In conclusion, it is evident that there exist widespread misconceptions and challenges in understanding when it comes to SaaS and the data protection challenges it poses. The perceptions we've examined in this chapter may initially seem reasonable, given the apparent convenience and promise of SaaS. However, when viewed under a microscope, they reveal dangerous pitfalls that businesses must avoid.

Believing that the organization does not rely heavily on SaaS, assuming that the SaaS vendor will protect all data, considering current backup vendors as adequate for SaaS data protection, claiming to be ransomware-proof, and conflating Single Sign-On with comprehensive data protection are all perceptions that, if left unchecked, can have dire consequences.

Organizations must wake up to the fact that we live in a SaaS-dominated world. As we've seen, even businesses that believe they use a modest number of SaaS services may be surprised to find that the actual number is much higher. This level of dependency requires a greater understanding and more sophisticated strategies for data protection.

Further, businesses must realize that while SaaS vendors do their part in protecting data, the responsibility for ensuring data safety is a shared one. Misplaced trust in SaaS vendors can lead to loss of critical data, disrupting business continuity and damaging reputations. An organization must take proactive steps to guard against such an eventuality.

Moreover, the assumption that certain existing backup solutions alone can provide adequate protection for SaaS data is a misconception. While these solutions can serve a powerful purpose, when combined in a tightly integrated manner, they can also provide the tools for a comprehensive data protection strategy for SaaS environments.

In the face of growing cybersecurity threats, companies cannot afford to be complacent, thinking that they are immune to ransomware attacks. Protection against such threats requires ongoing vigilance, updated cybersecurity measures, and robust backup and recovery solutions.

Challenging these perceptions is not just about correcting misunderstandings; it's about sparking a paradigm shift in how businesses approach SaaS data protection. The understanding and knowledge shared in this chapter can help businesses recognize their blind spots and, in turn, better prepare them to face the inherent challenges that come with the use of SaaS.

In the next chapter, we'll continue this journey towards better SaaS data protection. We'll turn our focus from identifying the misconceptions to discussing the solutions. We'll explore how to shape perceptions about these solutions, scrutinize various options available, and provide practical guidance on selecting the right approach that aligns with an organization's specific needs. Stay tuned as we delve deeper into the strategies and technologies that can help safeguard your SaaS data in an increasingly interconnected world.

Are you prepared to recover from a ransomware attack?

Scan this QR code to find out what your R-Score is today!

CHAPTER 6

The Dawn of a New Era in Data Protection

The SaaS Data Protection Dilemma

There's no denying that SaaS has revolutionized the way businesses operate. By offering solutions that are easily accessible, highly scalable, and relatively cost-effective, SaaS has undoubtedly become an integral part of our everyday lives. But as with every innovation, it brings its unique set of challenges. In this case, it's the issue of data protection.

As the CEO of HYCU, I've seen first-hand the struggle businesses face when it comes to protecting their data in the SaaS environment. With over 17,000 SaaS services being utilized in the United States alone, and the average company incorporating around 200 different combinations of these services into their operations, the scope of the problem is truly immense. The permutations and combinations of these SaaS services used across different departments, teams, and even individuals within a company create a complex web that's nearly impossible to unravel and protect effectively.

We've seen the shortcomings of traditional data protection solutions in this rapidly evolving digital landscape. These solutions, built for a time when data was more centralized and less diversified, struggle to keep up with the dynamic and ever-expanding world of SaaS. The traditional methods of protecting data on a few central servers are proving to be inadequate in an era where data is dispersed across a multitude of SaaS platforms.

The problem is not just the sheer number of SaaS services but also the unique data protection needs of each service. Every SaaS application has its data structures, user rights management, and mechanisms for data transfer and storage. Devising a customized data protection solution for each of these services is, from a practical standpoint, a Herculean task. And even if such tailored solutions were created, managing them would be a logistical nightmare.

This is where the traditional approach to data protection reaches its limit. The concept of building bespoke data protection solutions for every possible combination of SaaS services in use by a company is mathematically and pragmatically infeasible. Moreover, even if such an ambitious project were feasible, it would consume enormous resources and create an operational headache for the organization. In short, traditional data protection methods are simply not cut out for the SaaS-dominated era we find ourselves in.

We find ourselves standing at a crossroads. The landscape of business data has changed dramatically, and our strategies for protecting this data need to change as well. But how can we devise a solution that's both comprehensive, capable of covering the plethora of SaaS services, and yet manageable, without becoming an operational burden?

This is the central challenge that we at HYCU have sought to address. It's a complex problem, no doubt, but it's one that we believe is solvable. And the solution lies not in an outdated paradigm of singularly tailored solutions but in an innovative, adaptable, and user-centric approach to data protection. In the following sections, I'll delve into our solution, R-Cloud, and how it represents a new era in SaaS data protection.

The HYCU Solution: R-Cloud, A New Era in SaaS Data Protection

The challenge was clear: we needed a data protection solution that could span across the vast landscape of SaaS services without becoming an insurmountable task. But how do we accomplish this feat? As we pondered on this, I remembered a piece of wisdom from one of my mentors, Veselin Jevrosimović. He said, "Simon, if you're going to be CEO of a company, you don't want to think for a thousand people. You want a thousand people thinking for you."

And it clicked. The idea was not for us to build data protection for the thousands of SaaS integrations. Rather, the strategy was to create a platform where these numerous SaaS services could easily integrate with HYCU. This year, we launched R-Cloud, the world's first development platform for data protection, built on this very premise.

With R-Cloud, we embraced the seemingly impossible task of data protection for 17,000 SaaS services. Instead of viewing it as a burden, we saw an opportunity: the chance to provide customers with more value than any other data protection vendor. By creating a platform that enables easy integration with any SaaS service, we empower our customers to protect their data, regardless of the combination of services they employ.

And we didn't stop there. We knew that just integrating these services wasn't enough. Customers needed a way to manage all that data, to visualize it in a clear and coherent manner. So, we incorporated what we call the R-Graph into R-Cloud.

R-Graph does more than just map out your SaaS services. It creates a vivid visual representation of all the SaaS services you have across your organization, almost like a tree. Each branch of the tree represents a different department, and each leaf signifies a distinct SaaS service in your company.

With R-Graph, you get a bird's-eye view of your SaaS environment. Every service you have is automatically discovered, mapped out on the tree, and labeled as either protected or unprotected. For the protected services, all the policies associated are visible. And for the unprotected ones, it's as easy as a click to add a marketplace integration to back up and recover all of that data.

The result is a comprehensive, yet straightforward solution that not only gathers all the critical data from your SaaS applications but also provides a neutral staging ground for protection. With R-Cloud, you can visualize, manage, and protect all your SaaS data under a single pane of glass.

So, is this our solution to the SaaS data apocalypse? Absolutely. It's not just a dream anymore – with R-Cloud, it's now possible. It takes the complexity of the SaaS environment and simplifies it, giving customers the ease of managing their data protection needs effortlessly. That's what we believe Gen 3 data protection should be – lightweight, modern, and future-proofed, continually evolving just like the SaaS landscape it aims to protect.

The Rise of Shadow IT: A Double-Edged Sword

The term "Shadow IT" refers to the systems, solutions, and procedures used within organizations without official approval. It emerged out of the need for departments to solve immediate problems without going through lengthy IT approval processes. On one hand, it drove innovation and agility. However, it also introduced a slew of risks. Sitting at a conference in New York, I distinctly remember a prominent CIO admitting to the sense of resignation many felt. Controlling Shadow IT seemed an impossible task. Granting departments more autonomy might have been a budgetary solution, but from a data protection perspective, it was a disaster waiting to happen.

The "Aha!" Moment: Birth of the Resilient Approach

When we embarked on the journey to develop our cloud platform at HYCU, we envisaged more than just another data protection solution. We envisioned a seismic shift in how businesses approached ransomware resiliency. As the world's pioneering multi-cloud data protection service, we aimed to not just protect data but to visualize it in ways that would be transformative for organizations. The objective was crystal clear: make data both visible and resilient, regardless of where it resided.

From Disbelief to Gratitude: The Market's Response

The real test of any product is in its reception. In our interactions with CISOs, CIOs, and IT heads of major organizations, the response was nothing short of remarkable. The prevailing emotions were disbelief, amazement, and, most hearteningly, gratitude. These reactions validated our conviction: there was a profound need for solutions that offered visibility and control amidst the increasing complexity of SaaS environments.

Our cloud platform is more than just a service; it's a philosophy. The "wait-and-see" approach towards managing data has its limitations. In today's digital landscape, waiting often results in loss—of data, revenue, and trust. Our platform empowers organizations to regain control, giving them the tools and insights, they need to manage their entire data estate, regardless of ownership or location.

The Brilliance of R-Graph: Translating Complexity into Simplicity

Within the expansive universe of SaaS services, data management emerges as a pivotal challenge. Traditional systems and protocols often fall short in their ability to seamlessly integrate, protect, and recover data from various SaaS applications. Recognizing this, we innovated our way to a ground-breaking solution: the R-Graph feature within R-Cloud.

R-Graph is not just another tool in the box; it's a revolution in how businesses perceive, interpret, and manage their data. The secret to its transformative power lies in its ability to distill a complex ecosystem of SaaS integrations into a clear, interactive, and visually engaging format—a tree-like structure.

Consider the tree as an analogy for your organization. Each branch represents a different department, and each leaf symbolizes a different SaaS service within that department. This structure allows for a natural and intuitive understanding of how your organization's data is distributed across various SaaS services.

But R-Graph goes beyond merely visualizing the SaaS environment. It uses intelligent algorithms to automatically discover all the SaaS services you have, mapping them out on the tree and labeling them as either protected or unprotected. This automated discovery and classification process eliminate the manual and often error-prone task of tracking data protection status across numerous SaaS services.

When it comes to the protected services, R-Graph provides an instant overview of all the associated policies. This functionality gives an added layer of transparency, ensuring that you have complete visibility into how your data is being secured.

For unprotected data, R-Graph offers a quick and easy solution. With just a click, you can add a marketplace integration that backs up and recovers all the data associated with that particular service. This effortless integration not only ensures comprehensive data protection but also empowers you to take control of your data security.

The culmination of these features positions R-Cloud with R-Graph as an all-encompassing solution for SaaS data management. From discovery to visualization, protection to recovery—everything can be managed under a single pane of glass. It eliminates the need for juggling multiple tools or platforms and provides a consolidated view of your entire data ecosystem.

In essence, R-Graph encapsulates the core principle that underlies all HYCU solutions—transforming complexity into simplicity. We acknowledge the inherent complexity of the SaaS environment and counter it with a solution that makes data management not just manageable but also intuitive.

R-Graph signifies a shift in the industry—away from traditional, compartmentalized data management systems towards more integrated, interactive, and user-friendly solutions. It is an affirmation of our commitment at HYCU to continually push the boundaries of innovation, redefining what's possible in SaaS data management. R-Graph truly takes data protection into the future—making it more accessible, understandable, and manageable for all.

The Lightning Pace of R-Cloud: Accelerating SaaS Data Protection

One of the defining features of the R-Cloud platform that sets it apart from traditional data protection solutions is its implementation speed. In a world where the volume of data is expanding exponentially, the ability to rapidly respond and adapt to changing environments is paramount. At HYCU, we've made it a priority to design our solutions to be agile, efficient, and incredibly fast to implement.

We stand at the precipice of a new era in SaaS data protection, powered by R-Cloud. Within the span of a year, we will complete a hundred SaaS integrations. While this is a significant milestone in its own right, it only marks the beginning of our journey. Our ultimate aim is to cover the top 500 services over the next few years. We don't deny that this is a formidable goal, but we believe it's an achievable one.

R-Cloud doesn't just promise swift implementation; it delivers it. To illustrate this point, imagine a potential customer deciding to use our service. They would simply need to navigate to rcloud.hycu.com, log in with their username and password, and almost instantaneously, they would be able to start organizing and protecting their SaaS services.

This instant access and immediate operability are emblematic of the true SaaS nature of our platform. There's no need to download anything or install any hardware, eliminating the cumbersome setup processes that typically accompany traditional data protection solutions. This speed of implementation doesn't just save our customer's time; it also ensures that they can start protecting their valuable data immediately, reducing their exposure to potential data losses.

One of the key tenets of SaaS is its ease of use, and R-Cloud epitomizes this characteristic. If you've ever used a SaaS service, you'll appreciate the simple and intuitive nature of these platforms. We've strived to emulate this experience in R-Cloud. Whether you're opening Adobe to create a design, Evernote to jot down an idea, or Zoom for a team meeting, the process is straightforward, and using our platform is no different.

In developing R-Cloud, our goal wasn't merely to mirror the typical consumer experience found in most SaaS platforms; we aimed to elevate it. And we believe we've achieved that with R-Cloud. For the first time in the data protection industry, you'll find a platform that seamlessly blends usability and functionality.

This unprecedented speed and simplicity of implementation aren't just features of R-Cloud; they define it. The promise of immediate data protection, the ease of integration, the absence of cumbersome setup processes - these are not just conveniences. They are game changers. They represent a significant leap forward from traditional data protection methods, placing HYCU firmly at the forefront of SaaS data protection innovation. With R-Cloud, we are not just keeping pace with the evolving SaaS landscape; we are setting the pace.

Revolutionizing the Market: HYCU's Commercial Model

The commercial model we've developed at HYCU for R-Cloud is a significant departure from traditional approaches in the data protection industry. It was designed with flexibility and simplicity at its core, bringing a breath of fresh air to a sector often characterized by convoluted pricing structures and rigid terms.

Our pricing model is built around the concept of simplicity. We charge a flat rate of a few dollars per integration per month. The calculation is straightforward, based on two key variables: the number of SaaS integrations protected, and the number of underlying users. This transparent and direct pricing eliminates the confusion that often accompanies the tiered pricing structures prevalent in the market. It allows our customers to understand exactly what they are paying for and how much it will cost, giving them a clear picture of their investment in data protection.

However, where our commercial model truly shines is in its flexibility. As organizations evolve, their SaaS ecosystem often changes, with users shifting between different services based on business needs. Most data protection providers don't accommodate this fluidity, locking customers into rigid contracts tied to specific SaaS platforms. In contrast, our pricing model gives our customers the freedom to move users between services as and when needed. This ensures they only pay for the protection they require, providing an efficient and cost-effective solution to data protection.

Our flexible approach is more than just a pricing strategy; it's a reflection of the SaaS ecosystem's dynamic nature. As companies pivot and adapt to the ever-changing business environment, their data protection needs to do the same. Our flexible pricing model is our response to this need, mirroring the fluidity of the SaaS environment in our offerings.

This commercial model sets us apart from other data protection providers in the market. Many legacy backup companies are still attempting to use outdated pricing models, selling by socket, by node, or even pushing hardware sales. These models may have been effective in the past, but they are ill-suited to the dynamic and scalable nature of SaaS. Our SaaS-native pricing model is designed to cater to these evolving needs, providing an innovative and flexible solution to data protection.

Furthermore, our commercial model embraces the scalability inherent in SaaS. Regardless of whether a customer has a handful of SaaS integrations or hundreds, our pricing model scales accordingly, ensuring that our service remains affordable and accessible for businesses of all sizes.

Our commercial model reflects our commitment to pioneering a new era of SaaS data protection. It's not merely a pricing strategy; it's a revolution in how we think about data protection. It represents our belief that data protection should be simple, flexible, and accessible, mirroring the ethos of the SaaS services it seeks to protect. At HYCU, we're not just adapting to the changes in the SaaS landscape; we're leading the charge.

Envisioning a World Fully Protected: HYCU's Ultimate Dream

Our dream at HYCU extends far beyond our technological achievements or our innovative commercial model. At its core, our dream is rooted in a singular, unshakeable belief: every business, irrespective of its size or sector, deserves comprehensive and accessible data protection.

The rise of SaaS has fundamentally reshaped the landscape of modern business operations, enhancing productivity, fostering collaboration, and accelerating innovation. Yet, this transition has also introduced new vulnerabilities, as businesses grapple with the complex challenge of safeguarding their data across a multitude of SaaS applications.

As a result, data protection has often been perceived as a complex, daunting task, fraught with technological intricacies and financial burdens. It's a perception that we at HYCU are determined to change. Our goal is not just to create advanced data protection solutions, but to make these solutions universally accessible, easy to use, and economical.

With the launch of R-Cloud and R-Graph, we believe we've made a significant leap toward that goal. R-Cloud is our solution to the challenging issue of data protection across a multitude of SaaS services. With R-Cloud, data protection is no longer a herculean task, but a manageable process that can be customized to each organization's unique needs.

However, effective data protection is more than just a technological solution. It's also about clarity, visibility, and control. That's where R-Graph comes in. With R-Graph, we've transformed the way businesses view and manage their data. No longer are businesses forced to navigate through a maze of data silos, uncertain about their data's security. Instead, R-Graph provides a clear, concise visualization of every SaaS service in use, highlighting the state of data protection in each.

Together, R-Cloud and R-Graph form a comprehensive data protection solution that not only tackles the complexity of protecting data across numerous SaaS applications, but also simplifies the process of managing and monitoring that protection. Yet, this is more than just a solution. It's a realization of our dream, a step towards a world where comprehensive data protection is not a luxury for a few, but a norm for all.

The path to this dream may be long and fraught with challenges. But we believe that it is a journey worth undertaking. The promise of a world where every business, large or small, can safeguard its data with ease and confidence is a promise worth pursuing. With every innovation, every solution, and every customer we serve, we come one step closer to that dream.

The journey may be long, but the destination is clear. Our dream is a world where the complexities of SaaS data protection are not an obstacle, but a manageable reality. A world where every business can confidently say, "Our data is protected." With R-Cloud and R-Graph, we believe that this world is not just a distant dream, but an achievable, tangible reality. We are here to make that dream come true.

Setting the Stage for a Deeper Dive

As we draw the curtain on this chapter, the complex landscape of SaaS data protection and the innovative solutions we've developed at HYCU - R-Cloud and R-Graph - have been unveiled. We have shared our dreams, our challenges, and our novel approach to tackling the complexities of SaaS data protection. We have unveiled a new perspective on the issue, illuminating the potential for a future where SaaS data protection is not an impossibility, but a manageable and seamless process.

In an era where SaaS solutions are the bedrock of business operations, the stakes are high, and the demand for effective, user-friendly, and affordable data protection solutions is undeniable. R-Cloud and R-Graph represent our contributions to this pressing demand, our vision of a world where every SaaS service, regardless of its size or complexity, can be effortlessly safeguarded.

However, the journey doesn't end here. The technology we've built and the commercial model we've designed may sound revolutionary, but their true potential can only be appreciated when we delve into the intricacies of how they address the issue at hand.

The next chapter aims to do precisely that. We will be taking a deep dive into the inner workings of our solution, uncovering the nuts and bolts of R-Cloud and R-Graph. From the instant a customer logs onto R-Cloud to the moment they visualize their data protection status using R-Graph, we will walk you through the journey, examining how our technology transforms the daunting task of SaaS data protection into a straightforward, manageable process.

We will also further explore our commercial model, highlighting its flexibility and accessibility. We understand that each business is unique, with diverse needs and varying financial capabilities. As such, our commercial model has been designed to accommodate these differences, ensuring that data protection is not only technologically accessible but financially feasible as well.

In taking this deep dive, our goal is not just to showcase our technological innovation or commercial flexibility. Rather, it is to bring to light the thought process, the principles, and the aspirations that underpin our solution. We believe that understanding these underlying aspects is essential to fully appreciate the value of R-Cloud and R-Graph.

So, as we step into the next chapter, let's prepare to delve deeper into the world of SaaS data protection, demystify the complexities, and explore the solution that we at HYCU believe is capable of transforming this challenging landscape. We will take a step-by-step journey through our solution, comprehending how we are turning the impossible into the possible, and making our dream of a world fully protected, a tangible reality.

Scan this QR Code to find out what SaaS data you may have unprotected with R-Graph.

CHAPTER 7

A Dream to be Realized – Managing Your IT in the SaaS Era

Many of us recognize the conventional workings of an IT department. Chances are, you know about your organization's infrastructure costs, the volume of data you oversee, the cloud services you utilize, and the brand names present in your data center.

However, when it comes to the multitude of SaaS services your company uses, the visibility significantly diminishes. You'd likely have to reach out to numerous colleagues to get an accurate overview. The key here is not just the number of SaaS services in use, but understanding and managing the data they create.

What we propose is a new approach that not only provides greater transparency but also better control over your data estate. Instead of struggling to visualize where all your data resides and how it's protected, our innovative solution will let you see your entire data estate in a matter of seconds. Imagine a real-time image representing your on-premises architecture with all its data, storage and servers. In the same overview, you can also see all of the public clouds you use, along with the different services running inside them.

This solution doesn't stop at providing a visualization; it takes things a step further. You will be able to see every SaaS service across your entire organization, scoring each one for relevance and usage. But the cherry on top is the ability to protect all this data and manage all of your compliance under a single pane of glass. It means consolidating your data protection policies across on-premises, public cloud, and SaaS, bringing them all under a unified, easy-to-manage system.

At this point, I want to emphasize that our vision goes beyond creating a pleasing visual representation of your data. It's about truly understanding your data estate, breaking down silos, and getting a comprehensive picture of your organization's SaaS services. Our approach helps you take stock of your data protection policies that you have in place across on-prem, public cloud, and SaaS.

A question we often get is why our solution is necessary when many businesses already have multi-cloud providers, such as AWS or Azure. Aren't these companies already offering the tools to understand and manage their data estate? Yes and no. While these providers offer tools for their respective platforms, the current state of play lacks an aggregate view of all the data that a business manages across different clouds and SaaS applications.

Think of it like this: If we were to map out a company's data estate, we might find Azure and AWS for cloud services, HP servers for on-prem, and maybe 150 different SaaS apps. They could be using different backup services like Druva for AWS or Veeam for Azure, and yet still, a large part of their data could be unprotected. This translates into managing multiple vendors, dealing with different screens and processes, and having to hire specialized personnel for each technology.

Our solution is to bring all these different workloads, data protection vendors, policies, people, training, resources, updates, and hardware configurations under one umbrella. We've designed a single, easy-to-manage SaaS service that lets you take control, giving you complete visibility of where all your data is and how it's protected.

When we look back at the history of data protection, we find solutions designed for specific environments, such as Veritas for UNIX, Commvault for Windows, Veeam for VMware, and so on. But none of these solutions catered to a multi-cloud environment. Recognizing this gap, we designed an "inverted platform." Instead of starting with a big platform designed for a specific environment, we built lightweight backup and recovery services for each environment (VMware, GCP, Azure, etc.) and then tied them together under one roof.

Our inverted platform also stands out for its extensibility. When we built this platform, we ensured it was designed to adapt and expand easily as we added new SaaS services or integrations. This design feature made our platform more akin to the iPhone – just like developers write apps to expand the iPhone's capabilities, anyone can add a certified integration to our platform, expanding its feature set.

When it comes to competition, while we do have competitors in each data silo, we don't have any in aggregate other than ourselves. This singular, unified approach to data management gives us a distinct advantage in the market.

Looking ahead, we see a future where businesses no longer need to grapple with data visibility and protection issues. A future where you can quickly and easily see where all of your data is and how it's protected. You can ensure that all of your company's data, no matter where it resides, is safeguarded under one comprehensive data protection strategy.

We believe that the data protection industry needs to evolve, much like the antivirus industry did. Just as antivirus providers consolidated under unified threat management (UTM), we foresee a future where businesses will consolidate their data protection under unified data management (UDM). This will not only provide companies with a full view of their data estate but also simplify compliance, governance, and discovery.

So, are you ready to turn the page and step into a new era of data management? Are you prepared to shed the fragmentation of multiple vendors and siloed solutions, and instead embrace a unified, simplified approach? The data landscape is vast and complex, but it doesn't have to be a nightmare to navigate.

We invite you to join us on this journey towards a more transparent, efficient, and controlled data estate. We're ready to assist you in reimagining your approach to data, breaking down barriers and providing you with the tools to better understand and control your data landscape.

We are revolutionizing the way businesses manage data, and we want you to be part of this transformation. So, let's do this together. After all, data is not just about storage and protection. It's a resource, a lifeline, the bedrock of your organization's operations and innovation. Let's treat it with the respect it deserves.

So, there you have it. Our mission is to take the nightmare of data sprawl, protection, and compliance and turn it into a dream of unified data management. Our vision is a world where businesses have complete control over their data, with full visibility and protection in a single pane of glass. This is more than just a product; it's a change in how we approach and value data.

We have the technology. We have the vision. All we need now is for you to join us on this journey. It's time to take back control of your data. It's time to make this dream a reality.

A Vision for the Future

Here at HYCU, we firmly believe in creating a future where data visibility and management no longer pose colossal challenges to businesses. Our solution offers a comprehensive platform to visualize and manage your entire data estate within moments. A world where your data management shifts from an intimidating conundrum to an empowering control center.

When we say, "your entire data estate," we truly mean it. Consider the sheer magnitude of what this means. We're talking about the ability to comprehend the intricate labyrinth of your on-premises architecture and data volume, all in one fell swoop. Rather than spending countless hours, resources, and mental bandwidth attempting to decipher the complex web of on-premises data, you can now observe it effortlessly in a simplified, visual format.

And that's just the beginning. The power of our solution extends far beyond the on-premises infrastructure. It traverses the sometimes-nebulous realm of the public cloud. It integrates all the data from various public clouds, and their respective services, into one accessible visual. Rather than having to navigate each cloud service separately, with our solution, you can now grasp the totality of your cloud data landscape at a single glance.

Now, let's talk about SaaS. It's become an integral part of most businesses, with many using a multitude of SaaS services across their entire organization. Tracking the data in these services often requires interfacing with numerous vendors and dashboards. We streamline this process by pulling together data from every SaaS service your company uses. It is no longer a Herculean task to get an overview. Instead, it's as simple as looking at a single screen.

But, as you well know, visualization is just one aspect of data management. The beauty of our solution is that it doesn't just give you a bird's eye view of your data estate but also places the controls firmly in your hands.

Our platform enables you to manage all of your data protection policies across various domains - be it on-premises, public cloud, or SaaS services - from one central place. Imagine a world where you can control, modify, and deploy data protection policies across your entire organization, without having to hop from one interface to another. It doesn't matter where your data resides, you can keep it protected using one single consolidated view. This unified approach significantly reduces the complexity and potential for error inherent in juggling multiple data management tools.

Moreover, this consolidation goes a long way in simplifying your data management. By offering an integrated solution that provides a complete picture of your data estate, we help eliminate the chaos that usually comes with managing data across various platforms. We replace it with a sense of calm control, with you firmly at the helm.

The future we envision is one where businesses have a comprehensive and unobstructed view of their data landscape. A future where data management is not a dreaded chore but a strategic asset that enhances business efficiency and security. This vision drives our commitment to create and deliver a solution that simplifies data visualization and management, giving businesses the power to truly own their data, no matter where it lives.

That's the future as we see it. A future where data management becomes a powerful asset instead of an uphill battle. And with HYCU, it's a future that's already within your grasp.

The Necessity of a Unified Approach

We live in an era where the business landscape is as much digital as it is physical. The rise in digital data generation and storage has necessitated a rethinking of how we manage and protect our data. Currently, the common practice involves using a myriad of backup products. This might sound efficient in theory, but in practice, it's quite the opposite. This traditional approach not only complicates operations but also inflates costs, and most troublingly, enhances the risk of data loss across platforms.

At HYCU, we challenge this status quo. Our solution is the embodiment of simplicity, efficiency, and robustness. We offer a single SaaS service to manage all of your data, regardless of its location - on-premises, public cloud, or within SaaS services. This comprehensive approach is not a mere convenience; it's a necessary evolution, an antidote to the complex, expensive, and risky data management practices in vogue.

Skeptics might dismiss this need for a unified approach, arguing that given the prevalence of multi-cloud adoption, businesses should already possess the means to know and manage their data estate. But the ground reality is a stark contrast. Rather than a cohesive, unified picture, the data landscape within most organizations is fractured and lacks central control.

Let's visualize a typical organization today. Picture them employing separate backup services for Azure, AWS, and physical servers. Add to this the additional layers of backup services needed to safeguard various SaaS services. What does this entail?

First, there are multiple vendors to manage. This scenario results in a constant juggle between different relationships, with each requiring separate contracts, negotiations, renewals, and management. It's not just cumbersome; it's a resource drain.

Secondly, the organization is left with numerous interfaces to monitor. Each platform has its own dashboard, its own peculiarities, and its own learning curve. Keeping an eye on all these separate interfaces is not only time-consuming but also increases the risk of oversight and mistakes.

Finally, there's a demand for specialized staff familiar with each platform. This requirement translates into a need for more extensive training or hiring specific expertise for each platform, adding to the company's operational costs and complexity.

Our solution at HYCU addresses all these challenges head-on. We wrap all these fragmented elements into one easy-to-manage service. The multiple vendors are replaced by a single provider - us. The numerous interfaces are consolidated into a single, user-friendly dashboard. The need for specialized staff is greatly reduced as our platform is designed with simplicity in mind, needing minimum training to operate efficiently.

In essence, we are redefining data management by replacing the multiple, siloed vendor relationships with a single, consolidated solution. Our unified approach simplifies data management operations, reduces associated costs, and most importantly, mitigates the risk of data loss across all platforms.

We believe that the future of data management is unified, simplified, and secure. This is not just a vision for us; it's a path we are paving for organizations worldwide. With HYCU, the future of data management is already here, and it is unified.

Bringing it all Together

The beauty of HYCU's solution lies in its comprehensiveness and simplicity. The path to unified data management isn't paved with complex algorithms, exhausting training programs, or a hodgepodge of services. Instead, it's one single, streamlined software solution that serves as the backbone of your organization's data management needs.

The cornerstone of our service is offering you visibility and control. It's about shining a light on the invisible, making sense of the data maze that your organization navigates every day. With HYCU, the hidden is made visible, and the complicated is simplified. The elaborate web of data sources, from on-premises servers to public clouds to SaaS services, can be visualized in one single pane of glass.

Our platform's real-time visualization capabilities provide you with a bird's eye view of your entire data landscape, irrespective of its geographical or digital location. Just as a commander-in-chief has real-time access to battlefield conditions, you too have instant access to the state of your data estate. This comprehensive view drastically simplifies the management process, enabling you to make strategic decisions based on up-to-date information.

Beyond providing a unified view, HYCU offers the capability to manage all your data protection policies across your on-premises environments, public cloud, and SaaS services. It's about putting the power back in your hands, to manage, protect, and optimize your data, all from one centralized hub. This consolidated approach ensures not only streamlined operations but also robust protection against potential data loss or breach.

Additionally, we understand that data is not static. It grows, shifts, and evolves with your business. As such, our solution is built to be dynamic, adapting to your ever-changing data environment. We offer customizable protection levels, allowing you to adjust settings as per your business needs and industry regulations.

Moreover, the HYCU platform is user-friendly, designed with the understanding that usability is as critical as functionality. We've consciously minimized the learning curve, ensuring your team can effectively operate the system with minimal training. This simplicity does not come at the cost of sophistication. Our platform packs a powerful punch, equipping your organization with top-tier, cutting-edge data management capabilities.

HYCU brings it all together. We encapsulate the multi-faceted, sprawling world of data management into one elegant, comprehensive solution. We offer a single SaaS service that replaces multiple vendors, simplifies data management, reduces costs, and most importantly, offers robust protection across all platforms.

We're not just simplifying data management; we're reimagining it. We believe in a future where data management is unified, simplified, and secure, a future where your organization has complete control over its data. That future is not a distant dream. With HYCU, it's your present reality.

Broadening the Landscape

Standing out amidst a sea of competition, HYCU is making waves through its innovative approach towards data management. While our contemporaries in the industry typically focus on individual platforms or specific data environments, HYCU took a step back, observing the bigger picture, the wider, multi-cloud world that businesses are now operating in.

It wasn't simply about providing a service; it was about conceptualizing a vision that could align with the rapidly evolving digital landscape. HYCU's premise was not to bind businesses with ten different backup services, each specialized for a different platform, creating unnecessary complications and redundancies.

Instead, we set out on a revolutionary path. We embarked on creating lightweight, nimble backup and recovery services for each platform, keeping them efficient yet effective. But our vision did not stop there. Our ingenuity lied in then tying all these individual services together, amalgamating them into a cohesive whole - what we now call our "inverted platform".

Why the term 'inverted', you may wonder? This term is reflective of our modus operandi. Instead of considering each platform in isolation, we have 'inverted' our perspective, focusing on the collective picture, the entirety of the multi-cloud environment.

A Design that Fosters Expansion

Guided by our unwavering commitment to extensibility, we designed our platform to be flexible and scalable. During the development process, we stumbled upon a groundbreaking revelation - our "penicillin moment." Our platform was ingeniously constructed to allow easy expansion for protecting new SaaS services or accommodating integrations without necessitating a rewrite of existing code. This design foresight effectively future proofs our solution, preparing it for the unknown landscapes of tomorrow's digital world.

Rather than being static, our platform was conceived as a dynamic, living system, capable of adapting and evolving to meet the demands of the constantly shifting data management landscape. The architecture of HYCU is fluid, flexible, and adaptable, mirroring the very nature of the data it handles.

With an ambition to democratize our platform, we decided to harness the collective power of a global development community. We're not merely encouraging, but actively facilitating crowdsourcing for the development of certified integrations. The analogy of HYCU as an iPhone resonates perfectly here, with developers across the globe being invited to 'write apps' that extend its functionality.

Just as the App Store transformed the iPhone from a mere communication device into a versatile, multifunctional tool, these crowd-sourced integrations have the potential to drastically extend the scope and efficacy of HYCU. It's about enhancing and personalizing the platform, enabling it to cater to a wider variety of specific use-cases and client needs.

Navigating the Competitive Landscape

In the dynamic and multifaceted world of data management, competition is inevitably rife. And yes, while we acknowledge the presence of competitors operating within individual data silos, when we zoom out and view the landscape in its entirety, we find ourselves in a unique position - one where competition is sparse, nearly nonexistent. This is not to say that there are no challenges. There are, but they come in less conventional forms.

Our true competition, if you can call it that, is not other companies, but rather the complacency that pervades many organizations. It's a complacency that leads them to overlook, or at times completely neglect, the vital task of protecting their SaaS data. We call this phenomenon the "big lie" – a misbelief that data stored in the cloud is inherently safe and immune to threats. This is a dangerous assumption, and one that organizations should be wary of falling into.

The cloud is not an invincible fortress. While it certainly provides an array of benefits such as scalability, accessibility, and cost savings, it's also susceptible to data breaches, losses, and other threats. The key to navigating this nuanced landscape is to be proactive and thorough in one's approach to data management. One cannot rely on assumptions or misconceptions; the stakes are simply too high.

Revolutionizing Preparedness with HYCU

In an effort to help organizations break free from this "big lie" and evaluate their true preparedness for data loss threats, HYCU has taken a proactive step. We've devised a simple, free tool that any organization can use to evaluate their data recovery abilities. This tool, available at getRscore.org, is designed to objectively assess an organization's readiness against one of the most insidious threats today - ransomware.

Ransomware, a form of malicious software designed to block access to a computer system until a sum of money is paid, has become a predominant threat in the digital world. According to a report by Cybersecurity Ventures, a new organization will fall victim to ransomware every 11 seconds with statistics emerging it will increase to every 2 seconds by 2031. These statistics are a stark reminder of the looming threat, highlighting the urgency of being prepared.

The getRscore.org test is more than just an assessment tool; it's a wake-up call, a reality check for organizations. It's designed to reveal any chinks in the armor, areas where you may be vulnerable. Once these vulnerabilities are identified, organizations can then take informed, targeted action to bolster their defenses, thereby reducing the risk of falling victim to ransomware attacks.

HYCU's aim is not to instill fear but to empower organizations. By providing them with the tools to understand and gauge their own readiness, we're enabling them to take ownership of their data protection strategies. It's about breaking down the "big lie", replacing complacency with vigilance, and transforming a seemingly complex task into a manageable one.

The call to action here is clear: Do not fall for the "big lie". Take advantage of our free test at getRscore.org to assess your readiness against ransomware. Remember, knowledge is power, and when it comes to protecting your data, you can never be too prepared. Let HYCU guide you in this endeavor, ensuring your data remains secure amidst a world of growing digital threats.

In essence, HYCU is redefining the way data management is viewed and executed. By focusing on a multi-cloud world, creating an adaptable inverted platform, and fostering a community-driven approach, HYCU stands apart from its competitors. Our platform is testament to our vision of a future where data management is efficient, unified, and above all, democratized. With HYCU, that future is not merely an aspiration, it's a working reality.

Securing the Future: A Glimpse into the Journey Ahead

Over the course of the rest of the book, we will peel back the layers of the data protection landscape, illuminating it with real-world case studies from mid-market companies who have secured their SaaS data with HYCU's technology.

These real-world case studies will not only serve to inspire but will also provide practical insights into how HYCU operates, bringing the abstract concepts we've discussed into tangible reality. Each case study will echo the sentiments of our journey together thus far, reinforcing the necessity of a unified, proactive, and comprehensive approach to data management.

The journey into these case studies is akin to stepping into a living laboratory. You'll see companies just like yours, grappling with similar challenges in their data management journeys. You'll witness firsthand the transformation these companies underwent as they adopted HYCU's solutions - the initial hurdles, the breakthrough moments, and the ultimate victories.

We'll delve into the stories of various mid-market companies, from different sectors and regions. Each one of these businesses had their unique data-related challenges – the volume of data, the complexity of managing numerous cloud and SaaS platforms, the fear of data loss, and the dread of potential ransomware attacks. Yet, despite the seeming diversity of their problems, they all found a solution in HYCU.

As we navigate these case studies, you'll discover how HYCU's unique approach to data management helped these businesses simplify their operations, reduce costs, mitigate risks, and, most importantly, gain a peace of mind knowing that their data was secure.

We will illustrate how HYCU, with its inverted platform design, accommodates the rapidly evolving world of cloud and SaaS platforms. The case studies will show how companies can easily expand and adapt their data management strategies with HYCU, keeping pace with technological advancements without the need to rewrite code or employ specialized staff.

This journey will reveal the power of a unified data management strategy in overcoming the complexities and threats of today's digital world. It will prove, through concrete examples, that the "big lie" - the notion that data in the cloud is inherently secure - is indeed a myth, and that proactive protection is not just a luxury, but a necessity.

Our journey ahead is rich, insightful, and empowering. As we traverse the landscapes of various businesses and their data management battles, we will arm you with knowledge, strategies, and confidence to face your own data management challenges.

So, as we transition from this introduction into the heart of the book, I invite you to join us on this journey. Whether you're an IT professional, a business owner, or simply someone interested in data management, there's something to be gleaned from the upcoming chapters.

As we proceed, remember the promise that HYCU holds for your organization - a promise of simplified, unified, and secure data management. Here's to a future where your data-related nightmares are turned into dreams, a future secured by HYCU.

Prepare to be enlightened, inspired, and empowered. Welcome to the world of HYCU. The future of SaaS data management awaits.

Are you prepared to recover from a ransomware attack?

Scan this QR code to find out what your R-Score is today!

CHAPTER 8

Averting the SaaS Data Apocalypse with the Boston Red Sox

In today's rapidly evolving digital landscape, we find ourselves immersed in the age of data proliferation. Every corner of the business world is inundated with a deluge of data from numerous cloud applications and systems. Among those navigating this intricate digital maze is the Boston Red Sox, one of baseball's most iconic teams.

Similar to the challenges faced by many modern companies, the Red Sox were not just dealing with one or two systems, but rather juggling an expansive ecosystem of technology. Every pitch, every cheer from the stands, every merchandise purchase, and every internal operational task culminated into myriad data points. Each of these points, representing a unique moment or transaction, were being continuously generated, meticulously saved, and frequently shared.

The sheer volume and variety of this data, while providing valuable insights and opportunities for enhancement, also presented potential pitfalls. Without the right strategies and safeguards in place, these data points could create vulnerabilities, exposing the organization to risks if not properly managed and protected. The context underscores the need for robust data management and cybersecurity measures to ensure the integrity and safety of the team's valuable digital assets.

Digital Complexity: The Red Sox's Quest to Secure a Thousand Applications

The digital era has brought forth numerous challenges for organizations, and the Boston Red Sox was no exception. Randy George, the Vice President of Technology Operations for this iconic baseball team, gave a detailed account of the intricate dynamics involved in managing the IT operations of a major league baseball entity.

One of the more pressing issues they encountered was taking the information gleaned from fingerprinting the number of SaaS applications visited with the 200 known applications in use. These applications spanned a wide range, from communication tools that facilitated internal conversations and coordination, to sophisticated CRM systems that tracked fan engagement and ticket sales. Every functional area of their vast operations was deeply embedded in the digital realm, and with this digitization came the unintended consequence of creating various data silos. Each application or system, while serving a critical purpose, often operated in isolation, making integrated data management and security an involved process.

While the Red Sox did benefit from an advanced centralized cybersecurity framework provided by Major League Baseball (MLB), they still faced a significant challenge. Their primary concern revolved around ensuring the security of a diverse array of both on-premises and cloud-based systems. These platforms, though essential for their operations, were scattered and disjointed, lacking a cohesive protective umbrella.

In essence, they urgently needed a comprehensive, holistic solution that would not only unify their various data streams but also bolster their data protection strategy against potential threats.

Unified Data Protection: HYCU Steps Up to Bat for the Boston Red Sox

Acting on a strong recommendation and backed by a previous fruitful engagement with MLB, the Boston Red Sox explored the offerings of HYCU. Initially, the team's focus was narrow, aiming at protecting their Google Cloud Platform (GCP) environment and ensuring the replication of their on-prem Dell Isilon cluster was seamless and secure. But as the dialogue deepened, it became clear that HYCU's potential to assist the Red Sox extended well beyond these initial touchpoints.

The intrinsic value HYCU brought to the table was its adaptive and integrative approach. The Boston Red Sox, with their vast expanse of technological tools, from CRM systems to communication platforms, found in HYCU a solution that could stretch across this gamut. HYCU's solution wasn't just a mere plug-and-play; it was tailored, adapting itself to diverse platforms. Whether it was ensuring data integrity on Office 365, maintaining robust security layers on Azure, or even managing SaaS applications like Okta and Atlassian, HYCU demonstrated unmatched versatility.

What set HYCU apart was its holistic approach to data protection. It wasn't just about creating barriers; it was about building an ecosystem where data could flow seamlessly, yet securely. And in doing so, it fortified the Red Sox's digital infrastructure, transforming HYCU into the organization's essential "Swiss Army knife" for navigating the intricate maze of modern data protection and management.

A Home Run in Data Security: Boston Red Sox's Game-Changing Strategy with HYCU and Okta

The modern digital age poses numerous challenges, but with the right partners, these challenges can transform into opportunities. This was precisely the case when the iconic baseball team, Boston Red Sox, teamed up with HYCU and Okta. The synergies each provided helped redefine how the Red Sox approached data security and management.

With Okta serving as the robust centralized identity pillar, it was HYCU's responsibility to ensure that the sprawling web of data across applications remained consistently safeguarded. The real challenge was not just to back up the data but to do it with precision, understanding the intricate dynamics of what needed protection the most and when.

Enter R-Graph, HYCU's innovative visualization tool. This feature didn't just provide the Red Sox with a passive, bird's eye view of their digital ecosystem. Instead, it actively illustrated, in real-time, the protective status of each of their Okta-integrated applications. Such clarity was invaluable. It allowed the Red Sox to discern which applications were shielded and which required immediate attention. This visual aid eliminated guesswork, letting the team strategically allocate resources, ensuring maximum protection based on an application's risk profile and organizational significance.

But the collaboration's success was not solely tethered to technology. It was the evolution in approach, facilitated by HYCU, which truly made a difference. The Red Sox weren't just employing a software solution; they were adopting a proactive approach to data management. With regular app reviews, risk assessments, and a dynamic backup strategy tailored to the unique demands of each application, the organization was not just reacting but preemptively securing its assets.

In pairing HYCU's comprehensive data protection capabilities with Okta's top-tier authentication services, the Boston Red Sox crafted a formidable dual-layered defense strategy. This approach not only fortified their digital infrastructure against potential threats but also ensured seamless business operations, even in the face of adversity.

"The amount of data we're taking in as a business now is mission critical. It's incredible for us to have a single data protection partner like HYCU for all of the disparate systems no matter where they all live. And, equally important is Okta, a centralized source of identity for all of our employees. For us, the joint technology is critical to us. Not a single day goes by where we're not adding one or two applications within Okta and being able to use HYCU for the data protection piece has been incredible for us. The biggest thing for us is we can sleep well at night knowing that all the data in our platforms is protected. Now we have a proper data protection and comprehensive approach for all our SaaS applications in place as well."

– Randy George, Vice President of Technology Operations, Boston Red Sox

Embracing a Unified Digital Future: Lessons from the Boston Red Sox

In the ever-complex space of digital data management, the Boston Red Sox have showcased how to transform challenges into opportunities. Their journey, detailed in this chapter, underscores the vital importance of proactive strategies and innovative partnerships to overcome digital challenges.

The partnership with HYCU and Okta wasn't just about employing state-of-the-art tools; it was about adopting a comprehensive, forward-thinking approach to data security. By merging HYCU's adaptable data protection capabilities with Okta's robust identity management, the Red Sox not only protected their vast digital assets but also streamlined their operations. This dual-layered defense strategy underscores the value of unifying fragmented systems under a cohesive protective umbrella.

Furthermore, 'R-Graph', HYCU's real-time visualization tool, highlighted the importance of active insights in modern data management. Such tools empower organizations to stay ahead, ensuring that they're not merely reactive but strategically preemptive.

Randy George's statement drives home the crux of the chapter: success in the digital age isn't just about integrating advanced technologies. It's about weaving them into the organizational fabric, ensuring legacy and innovation thrive together. As businesses look to the future, the Boston Red Sox's data strategy, rooted in unification and proactive defense, serves as a gold standard.

Scan this QR code to watch the interview with Randy George, Vice President of Technology Operations, Boston Red Sox.

CHAPTER 9

Averting the SaaS Data Apocalypse with Zebra Technologies

Zebra Technologies is more than just a familiar name in the SaaS industry; it represents innovation, adaptability, and a relentless pursuit of excellence. With roots deep in tech evolution, Zebra's legacy has been consistently marked by its ability to foresee market needs and pivot its strategies accordingly. As the world shifted towards cloud solutions and digital transformation became the mantra for businesses, Zebra was quick to adapt and take a leap into the future.

Zebra embarked on its cloud journey. Zebra's commitment to modernizing its suite of SaaS products has been extraordinary. From acquiring new technologies to optimizing existing ones, their progress reflects a conscious effort to deliver the best to their customers and stay ahead of the curve.

As Zebra grew both organically and through acquisitions, the volume and variety of their data grew exponentially. This influx of data, combined with their aggressive migration strategy needed tools that meet their needs.

Tackling Cloud Challenges Together: The HYCU-Zebra Synergy

When Zebra Technologies embarked on its dynamic transition to the cloud, our team at HYCU took pride in offering solutions that genuinely matched their needs. One of the pivotal reasons Zebra gravitated towards us was our agentless approach and the sheer ease with which our platform could be integrated. Our team, understanding the unique challenges faced by Zebra, tailored features to meet their demands, particularly the ability to snapshot databases. This precision-driven customization empowered Zebra to smoothly shift their databases between varied environments.

At HYCU, we've always envisioned offering clarity on where data resides and ensuring its protection. This perspective has been indispensable for a company of Zebra's stature, which has grown in multifaceted ways. By providing a consolidated viewpoint of their vast array of SaaS offerings, we believe we're aiding in streamlining their operations, ensuring efficiency, and paving the way for continued growth.

The SaaS industry is teeming with solutions, each promising to be the 'next big thing'. However, Zebra's choice to work with HYCU was rooted in a shared vision and a commitment to excellence. HYCU's expertise in data protection and its state-of-the-art technology stack set it apart from other vendors along with the opportunity to co-create and innovate solutions tailored to Zebra's unique needs.

Zebra Technologies' emphasis on our agentless technology, our flexibility to quickly bring new features to the market, and our receptiveness to integrate customer feedback into our roadmap underscores the depth and mutual respect of this relationship. It's a journey that transcends mere product utilization; it's about collaborative growth, mutual adaptation, and the unwavering commitment of both parties to deliver their best.

Accelerated Progress: The Tangible Outcomes

When HYCU was integrated into Zebra Technologies' operational infrastructure, the results were nothing short of transformative. One of the most notable impacts was the accelerated pace at which Zebra could now clone or replicate their databases. Processes that previously spanned days were now executed in mere hours. This substantial time-saving measure not only improved operational efficiency but also catalyzed smoother workflows and faster decision-making.

Zebra also appreciated HYCU's ability to support Google Native technologies and how it was indicative of a deeper trend: the evolving nature of SaaS partnerships. As Zebra leans further into these platforms, it underscores a promising horizon of continued mutual growth, shared innovation, and a commitment to harnessing the best of what technology offers.

Zooming out to view the larger picture, the collaboration between Zebra and HYCU serves as a case study for SaaS enterprises worldwide. It sheds light on how, with the right technological partnership, businesses can adeptly navigate the challenges presented by today's complex data terrain. By embracing innovative solutions like those offered by HYCU, companies aren't merely adapting; they are thriving, evolving, and setting new benchmarks in a tech world that never stands still.

"From the outset of our collaboration with HYCU, we recognized a synergy that went beyond mere vendor-client dynamics. HYCU's solutions have not only streamlined our processes but have also empowered Zebra to conquer challenges in the modern data landscape with confidence. Their commitment to understanding our unique needs and adapting their solutions accordingly is commendable. Our journey into the cloud has been made significantly smoother thanks to HYCU's innovative tools and dedicated team."

– Rama Gudhe, Senior Director of Cloud Operations, Zebra Technologies

Navigating the SaaS Landscape: The Triumph of Zebra Technologies and HYCU Collaboration

In an era marked by rapid technological progress, Zebra Technologies stands out not merely as a leader in the SaaS industry, but as a beacon of adaptability, innovation, and unyielding drive for excellence. HYCU's work with Zebra emerges not only as a success story but as a guidepost for other enterprises aiming to chart a path through this ever-evolving terrain.

HYCU, with its deep understanding of Zebra's unique challenges, offered more than just a point product. The company provided a symbiotic relationship, anchored in a shared vision and mutual respect. HYCU's agentless technology and nimble approach to feature development emerged as crucial factors in Zebra's decision to work with HYCU. Yet, more than that, it was the ethos of co-creation, of building solutions collaboratively, that truly set this alliance apart.

The tangible benefits are hard to overstate. With the integration of HYCU into Zebra's infrastructure, processes that were once time-consuming became almost instantaneous. This acceleration resulted in not only enhanced operational efficiency but also a more agile, nimble approach to decision-making. As Rama Gudhe, Senior Director of Cloud Operations at Zebra Technologies, observed, our work together went beyond traditional vendor-client dynamics, symbolizing a true meeting of minds.

Yet, this isn't just a standalone success story. It offers broader lessons for the SaaS industry. Firstly, it underlines the importance of selecting technology partners not just based on product offerings, but also on shared vision, adaptability, and a commitment to mutual growth. Secondly, it showcases the immense potential of collaborative innovation in addressing complex, multifaceted challenges.

In conclusion, the journey of Zebra Technologies and its collaboration with HYCU serves as a testament to the power of strategic alliances in the tech world. At a time when businesses across the globe grapple with the challenges of digital transformation and cloud transition, the Zebra-HYCU synergy offers a beacon of hope. It reminds us that with the right alliance, businesses can not only navigate the choppy waters of modern data management but can also set new standards of excellence, drive innovation, and pave the way for a brighter, more interconnected future.

Scan this QR code to watch the interview with Rama Gudhe, Senior Director of Cloud Operations, Zebra Technologies

CHAPTER 10

Averting the SaaS Data Apocalypse with Bain Capital

The 21st century heralded the era of digital transformation, and at its heart lies the rapid growth and adoption of SaaS. Today, companies ranging from startups to giants have adopted the agility and convenience of SaaS, transforming their operations and achieving a level of flexibility that was once unthinkable. However, as with every silver lining, there's a cloud, and in this context, it's a cloud of potential vulnerabilities.

Many companies, entranced by the allure of "the cloud," are lulled into a false sense of security. They believe their data is impervious to threats, simply because it's housed off-premises in these ethereal data centers. The misconception is dangerous. Just because data is out of sight doesn't mean it's out of harm's way.

This brings us to Bain Capital. Renowned as an esteemed global private investment firm, Bain Capital, with its extensive portfolio and footprint, wasn't one to wear rose-tinted glasses when it came to cloud security. They recognized the pitfalls and complexities inherent to this digital transition. The digital sprawl, if not managed appropriately, could lead to detrimental data breaches, potentially compromising the integrity of their investments and operations. And so, with the foresight that has always marked their strategic moves, Bain Capital chose to prioritize their data protection strategy.

Navigating the Digital Maze: Bain Capital's Quest for Data Visibility

In the dynamic landscape of global investment, firms like Bain Capital are not just players; they're front-runners. Their stakes span across a spectrum of industries and geographies, painting a vivid picture of diversification. This means their digital footprint isn't just large; it's multifaceted. With a vast and varied digital presence, Bain Capital found itself on the cutting edge of technological integration, leveraging a plethora of SaaS platforms. Each of these platforms was adeptly chosen to fulfill distinct business needs, be it CRM, supply chain management, data analytics, or any of the myriad functions a global entity requires.

However, such diversification, while offering operational agility, posed a significant challenge. The more the platforms, the more were the data silos – isolated repositories with their own configurations, storage mechanisms, and security protocols. In many cases, these protocols were either non-existent or starkly different from one another. This heterogeneity meant that not only was data scattered, but its protection mechanisms varied wildly.

Mark Sutton, Chief Information Security Officer (CISO) at Bain Capital, couldn't have encapsulated the challenge more succinctly. "It's not just about constructing walls around our assets; it's about first knowing where each brick is," he often remarked. The essence of his observation was simple yet profound: How does one safeguard assets that remain elusive? If data protection is akin to a jigsaw puzzle, then visibility is that crucial corner piece without which the entire picture remains incomplete.

But achieving this visibility was no walk in the park. The multitude of platforms can provide a double-edged sword. On one hand, they empowered Bain Capital with operational robustness; on the other, they could obscure the very assets they supported. The task of data protection, thus, transformed from a structured process to something akin to finding a needle in a haystack. And each haystack was different, with its own unique set of challenges and intricacies.

In this era of cyber vulnerabilities, such a scenario is sub-optimal. It isn't merely about losing data but about compromising the integrity of operations, credibility, and trust.

Illuminating the Shadows: HYCU's Revolutionary Approach to Data Visibility

As Bain Capital approached HYCU, one of their portfolio companies, it was clear they were in search of more than just a solution; they wanted a collaborator that shared their profound vision for robust data security. That's where HYCU was able to help and help illuminate even the murkiest depths of the digital world.

Built on the profound understanding that visibility is the cornerstone of protection, HYCU operates under a simple yet profound mantra: "If you can't see something, you can't protect it", echoing Mark's sentiments precisely. Through HYCU's cutting-edge visualization techniques, the team at Bain Capital was able to get a panoramic perspective on every single one of their data silos. It wasn't merely about identifying vulnerabilities - it was about comprehending the entirety of their digital ecosystem to guarantee a comprehensive shield.

In the realm of SaaS, many organizations mistakenly equate it with mere cloud workspaces. However, HYCU's methodology sharply distinguishes between the two. While cloud environments might offer a veneer of simplicity, the world of SaaS often comprises complex matrices of data interconnections. Our primary objective was to guarantee that Bain Capital was not only safeguarded, but also primed for prompt and smooth data recovery, irrespective of the evolving threat landscape.

A Digital Renaissance: The Tangible Transformation at Bain Capital Post-HYCU Integration

In the wake of the collaboration with HYCU, the transformation was both profound and powerful:

1. **Mastery over Data Landscape:** The Bain Capital team is now armed with unparalleled insights and granted proactive control. They were also able to meticulously monitor and manage every single one of their data repositories, effectively removing possible blind spots.

2. **Swift and Smooth Operations:** With HYCU's tailored backup and recovery blueprints, Bain Capital's data management gained heightened efficiency. Downtimes became virtually negligible, safeguarding against potential data loss and ensuring continuity in operations.

3. **Building the Digital Fortress:** With a granular understanding of their data topology, Bain Capital was able to amplify their defenses. Each data silo, regardless of its size or significance, was fortified with precision, making their digital environment an impenetrable bastion against threats.

"Transitioning to a digital ecosystem presented us with unprecedented challenges, especially in the realm of data visibility and security. When we collaborated with HYCU, we weren't just embracing a solution; we were welcoming a change catalyst. Their platform didn't just provide visibility in our data landscape—it helped with the transformation we were already making. From removing blind spots to ensuring prompt recovery, the transformation has been significant. It's rare to find a technology partner that understands your challenges as keenly as HYCU does, and HYCU has proven to be that invaluable ally for us at Bain Capital. Our data integrity, security, and management are in good hands, and for that, we're immensely grateful."

– Mark Sutton, CISO Bain Capital.

Embracing Visibility: Navigating the Future of SaaS with Clarity and Confidence

The rapid ascent of SaaS has unquestionably revolutionized the digital landscape, ushering in unparalleled conveniences and operational agility for businesses globally. Yet, as the narrative of Bain Capital poignantly underscores, this brave new world is not without its treacherous chasms of vulnerability. The very essence of SaaS—its decentralized, multifaceted nature—while transformative, can simultaneously obfuscate the clarity with which businesses perceive and secure their invaluable data assets.

Bain Capital's transformation serves as a good example and, more importantly, an illuminative guide for enterprises worldwide. The challenges they faced are not unique; in an age of digital sprawl, many organizations find themselves ensnared in a perplexing web of data visibility. What also sets Bain Capital apart is their proactive acknowledgment of the challenge and their pursuit of a robust solution. Their collaboration with HYCU helps accentuate the paramount significance of visibility in the realm of data protection. It's a powerful testament to the fact that, in the world of digital security, seeing is not just believing—it's safeguarding.

HYCU's approach to data visibility is both revolutionary and timely. In offering a panoramic, granular view of Bain Capital's digital ecosystem, it equipped them with the tools to not just react, but to preemptively shield themselves against potential threats. Such proactive data management strategies will undoubtedly become the gold standard in the coming years, as more enterprises recognize the intricacies of the SaaS environment.

Mark Sutton's testimonial captures the essence of this partnership, highlighting the invaluable nature of a solution that not only addresses present concerns but also anticipates future challenges. It's a resonant reminder of the symbiotic relationship between innovation and protection in the digital age. As businesses continue to evolve, so must their protective measures, ensuring they remain a step ahead of potential vulnerabilities.

In retrospect, the journey of Bain Capital and HYCU encapsulates the broader narrative of the 21st-century digital era—a tale of transformative possibilities, imminent challenges, and the enduring importance of vigilance. As companies globally navigate their own SaaS trajectories, this chapter offers a beacon, signaling both the pitfalls to avoid and the strategies to embrace. The 'SaaS Data Apocalypse' is not an inevitability; with foresight, collaboration, and innovative solutions like HYCU, businesses can continue their digital odysseys with confidence and security.

Scan this QR code to watch the interview with Mark Sutton, Chief Information Security Officer (CISO) at Bain Capital.

An Unwavering Commitment to Uptime and Data Protection

As I reflect on the journey of HYCU, our unwavering commitment to our mission becomes the unmistakable driving force behind our meteoric rise in the world of backup and data protection services. Launching HYCU in April of 2018, we embarked with a clear yet ambitious objective: to build a safer world. We recognized that the challenge of this digital age was not merely the sheer volume of data but rather the fragmentation of data across hundreds of silos, further exacerbated by the explosion of Software as a Service (SaaS).

My team and I envisioned a solution where users could see, manage, and protect all their data from one singular platform. Whether on-premises, in public clouds, or within SaaS platforms, we desired to centralize all data management. We sought to eliminate the chaos and complexity typical of scattered data storage and protection, a task as daunting as it was necessary.

Data protection's importance has never been more pronounced, especially given the rising threat of ransomware attacks. We understood that data, left vulnerable, could be weaponized and used against both individuals and organizations. Thus, HYCU's mission extended beyond merely offering a data management solution; it became a safeguard against the digital world's lurking threats.

Today, as I look back, my pride in our team is boundless. From humble beginnings, HYCU now serves over 3,600 customers across 78 countries. But this is merely the start of a journey reflecting a vision not just for selling a product but for embodying a philosophy. A philosophy committed to building a safer world through simplified data management and enhanced protection, meeting challenges head-on, and innovating continuously.

Our achievements are a testament to our relentless determination and innovative spirit. Yet we're not stopping here. The future brings new challenges and opportunities, and HYCU stands ready to continue shaping data protection's future. Confident in our ability to grow, adapt, and deliver, we remain steadfast in our mission: a safer world, one byte at a time.

HYCU's Legacy: A Vision of Resilience Against the Scourge of Ransomware

Legacy, often a mixed term in technology's fast-paced world, takes on a profound meaning for HYCU. Not about stagnation or past achievements, HYCU's legacy represents the mark it strives to leave on the world, shaping the future in the face of the menacing threat of ransomware.

HYCU's response to ransomware's challenges is comprehensive and groundbreaking. We've embarked on a mission to redefine how the world approaches this threat, focusing on enabling enterprise-grade data protection for any service. Our universal solutions protect data wherever it resides, creating a robust defense against ransom attempts and changing the ransomware game.

Our legacy aspiration is one of innovation, resilience, and impact. It's about altering perceptions, showing that legacy isn't about anchoring to the past but forward-thinking vision. In HYCU's context, legacy is battling ransomware at the forefront, developing solutions that address and eradicate the problem.

HYCU's legacy is more than technology; it resonates with universal aspirations for safety, security, and progress. As ransomware has become a "massive scourge," HYCU's vision shines as a beacon of hope. By ensuring data resiliency and fostering a culture of accessible and universal enterprise-grade data protection, we're shaping a more secure digital future for all.

In "Averting the SaaS Data Apocalypse," our journey through the treacherous landscape of data management and looming digital threats offers lessons, insights, and visionary approaches. HYCU's legacy, along with industry pioneers' stories and strategies, serves as both a beacon and a challenge, calling us to innovate, adapt, and rise.

May this book inspire all committed to shaping a future where the SaaS Data Apocalypse is not a looming disaster but a triumph story. A story we write together, one byte at a time.

Bibliography

11 Seconds. (2021). Retrieved from Infimasec: https://infimasec.com/blog/11-seconds/

Anthem Security Breach. (2015). Retrieved from ID Strong: https://www.idstrong.com/sentinel/anthem-security-breach/#:~:text=In%20the%20Anthem%20Data%20Breach,to%20Anthem's%20database%20of%20information.

BBC. (2020). Retrieved from Garmin begins recovery from ransomware attack: https://www.bbc.com/news/technology-53553576

Blackbaud to Pay $3 Million Over 'Erroneous' Breach Details. (2020). Retrieved from Bank Info Security: https://www.bankinfosecurity.com/blackbaud-to-pay-3-million-over-erroneous-breach-details-a-21410

CNA Paid $40 Million to Ransom. (2019). Retrieved from Bloomberg: https://www.bloomberg.com/news/articles/2021-05-20/cna-financial-paid-40-million-in-ransom-after-march-cyberattack

Colonial Pipeline Shuts. (2021). Retrieved from CNBC: https://www.cnbc.com/2021/05/08/colonial-pipeline-shuts-pipeline-operations-after-cyberattack.html

Data Privacy White House Government. (2022). Retrieved from White House Gov: https://www.whitehouse.gov/ostp/ai-bill-

of-rights/data-privacy-2/#:~:text=The%20American%20
public%20should%20be%20protected%20via%20built-in%20
privacy,%2C%20informed%2C%20and%20ongoing%20way.

Factsheet, Wannacry. (2018). Retrieved from CISA:
https://www.cisa.gov/sites/default/files/FactSheets/NCCIC%20
ICS_FactSheet_WannaCry_Ransomware_S508C.pdf

*FBI investigating ransomware attack affecting Eastern
Connecticut Health Network, Waterbury HEALTH.* (2023).
Retrieved from WTNH: https://www.wtnh.com/news/
connecticut/manchester-memorial-hospital-diverting-
emergency-patients-amid-technical-issues/

*Gartner Magic Quadrant for Enterprise Backup and Recovery
Software Solutions .* (2023). Retrieved from HYCU: https://www.
hycu.com/download/gartner-magic-quadrant-for-enterprise-
backup-and-recovery-solutions-2023

GitLab suffers major backup failure after data deletion incident.
(2017). Retrieved from TechCrunch: https://techcrunch.
com/2017/02/01/gitlab-suffers-major-backup-failure-after-
data-deletion-incident/

Global Cyber Outlook. (2023). Retrieved from World Economic
Forum: https://initiatives.weforum.org/global-cyber-outlook/
home

Hybrid Security Trends. (2023). Retrieved from Netwrix: https://
www.netwrix.com/2023_hybrid_security_trends_report.html

Is the Cloud secure? (2019, October 10). Retrieved from Gartner:
https://www.gartner.com/smarterwithgartner/is-the-cloud-
secure

Key Findings SaaS Management. (2022). Retrieved from Zylo: https://zylo.com/blog/key-findings-from-zylos-2022-saas-management-index/

Malware Bytes. (2020). Retrieved from Malware Bytes: https://www.malwarebytes.com/blog/news/2020/07/threat-spotlight-wastedlocker-customized-ransomware

Number SaaS Companies Statatistics. (2023). Retrieved from Ascendixtech: https://ascendixtech.com/number-saas-companies-statistics

Odaseva. (2022). Retrieved from SaaS Data Was the Target of 51% of Ransomware Attacks in the Last 12 Months; More Than Half of These Attacks Were Successful: https://www.odaseva.com/news-post/saas-data-was-the-target-of-51-of-ransomware-attacks-in-the-last-12-months-more-than-half-of-these-attacks-were-successful/

PwC. (2017). *Operation Cloud Hopper: What You Need to Know.* Retrieved from PwC: https://www.pwc.co.uk/cyber-security/pdf/pwc-uk-operation-cloud-hopper-report-april-2017.pdf

Solar Winds Attack. (2023). Retrieved from Tech Target: https://www.techtarget.com/whatis/feature/SolarWinds-hack-explained-Everything-you-need-to-know

Thank You

Thank You For Reading My Book!

I really appreciate all of your feedback, and I love hearing what you have to say.

I need your input to make the next version of this book and my future books even better.

Please leave me a helpful review on Amazon letting me know what you thought of the book.

Thank you so much!
Simon Taylor

Made in United States
North Haven, CT
30 September 2023

42203255R00104